THE HIGHLY SENSITIVE EMPATH

A PRACTICAL SURVIVAL GUIDE TO ACHIEVE COMPLETE EMOTIONAL, PHYSICAL, AND SPIRITUAL HEALING FOR EVERY PERSON

QUINN ROWE

© **Copyright 2019 - All rights reserved.**

Without direct written consent from the author or publisher, the material contained in this book may not be reproduced, duplicated, or transferred.

Under no conditions shall the publisher

or author be held responsible for any damages, reparations, or financial loss as a result of the data contained in this book. Either directly or indirectly.

Legal Notice:

This book is shielded by copyright. This book is for private use only. Without the author or publisher's approval, you may not modify, distribute, sell, use, quote, or paraphrase any portion of the material in this book.

Disclaimer Notice:

For instructional and leisure reasons only, please note the data contained in this document. Every effort was made to present full, precise, up-to-date, and reliable data. There are no declarations or implied warranties of any kind. Readers recognize that the author isn't involved in providing legal, economic, medical, or professional advice. The content of this book was obtained from different sources. Before trying any methods described in this book, please consult a certified professional.

By reading this paper, the reader agrees that the writer isn't liable under any conditions for any direct or indirect damages resulting from the use of the data contained in this paper, including, but not restricted to,— mistakes, omissions or inaccuracies.

INTRODUCTION TO EMPATHY

In a world where emotions have often been associated with weakness, it can be pretty tough coping in society if you're an empath. It's even worse when (like I used to be) you don't even know you're an empath, because often what happens is you invariably find yourself trapped in emotions, relationships, or environments that suck the life out of you.

Dealing with your emotions (and those of others) in a world that doesn't appreciate or value your sensitivities can be overwhelming and very detrimental to your wellbeing. There's a real sense of suffocation and powerlessness that accompanies this challenge which must be addressed and dealt with as early on in life as possible; otherwise, happiness becomes a daunting task.

This book and all the information contained is made for the sole purpose of helping you, the reader, finally come to a new understanding of what it means to be an Empath.

Sure you've seen a lot of people talk about it. Both science and spirituality seem to have strong concepts around what it means to be an empath. But you know what? In the end, only an empath can fully understand what it feels like to go through daily human living as such. And as far as I can see, there i'sn't much knowledge given in the way of navigating this path of being an empath successfully. At best, we find material that seems to increase confusion or promote a lifestyle that feels isolating and unsatisfying.

So if like me you want to enjoy life to the fullest while still honoring the subtle differences that enable you to perceive human living through a different lens, then may this book aid you in meeting that end.

Here's what this book isn't:

Before we get started here's some clarity regarding what you can expect from reading this book and what it won't be about. This isn't about some gendered nonsense isolating one from the other as I find that to be utterly unnecessary since research in HSP (highly sensitive people) shows that there's no difference between men and women.

It will neither excuse nor encourage inexcusable behavior, and it's not about elevating empaths over "normal" people. I've no interest in seeing you live an isolated life, and I certainly don't want to aid you in "avoiding" anything that would promote a healthier, happier human experience. I feel you already know all too well what to avoid. You certainly don't need my help with that!

But what you probably need is greater clarity on how you can enrich your life and stretch beyond the current comfort zone that abstracts the freedom you can feel in burning up your heart.

This is my intention in writing this book. If you resonate with the idea of overcoming the limitations that society often places on those of us who are highly sensitive and gifted with empathic abilities, then it's time for us to begin this journey.

Pace yourself. Trust in this full course and know that

you'll emerge more fearless, and empowered if you open-mindedly absorb the ideas contained in each chapter.

Shall we begin?

CHAPTER 1: THE DIFFERENCE BETWEEN EMPATHY AND BEING AN EMPATH

"When you begin to develop your powers of empathy and imagination, the whole world opens up to you."

- Susan Sarandon.

Empathy is a trait that can be learned by anyone. And to some extent, we all practice empathy in varying degrees as we interact with each other. But showing empathy and being an empath aren't identical.

Here's how to process the difference between the two.

Imagine you're sitting down at Starbucks with two

of your friends that you very much adore. Both strong in character and while different in personalities, you know they both have big hearts.

Suddenly a couple sitting next to you cause a scene. The guy bangs the table in anger spilling a perfectly wonderful Frappuccino all over and yells a few words before stomping out. The woman left behind feels utterly crushed and embarrassed. Tears stream down her red cheeks, and she hangs her head as low as possible as she quickly tries to clean up the mess created. For a moment, all eyes are on her, and you could feel everything that she felt.

One of your friends turns to you and asks, "Should we go over there and see if we can help?" As you look over to your friend, you notice her cheeks are flushed, and her eyes are just as teary as yours. It's almost as if you're both experiencing what the couple experienced. Before you can even respond, your other friend jumps in and says, "Naaa, she'll be fine. Look she's already stopped crying. Let it go."

What just happened in that scenario?

One of your friends did show some empathy and recognized the discomfort of the woman, but that's as far as it went. She was glad to get on with her day as if nothing happened. The other friend, however, seemed to have had a completely different experience. Her entire body chemistry changed. And you felt it too, didn't you?

This is the subtle difference between showing empathy and being an empath.

Empathy is the ability to understand and share the feelings of another. With a little conscious effort, every human being can demonstrate empathy when the situation calls for it.

When one is an empath, however, it's an entirely different experience. It's more like having an elevated gift and an ability to step into another person's shoes. An empath has the power to step outside his or her own experience and understand what another person is saying, thinking, and feeling. It's more than just being a highly sensitive person, and it goes beyond sensing emotions.

According to science, empaths are highly sensitive and can process emotions faster and more intimately. The common acronym for this is HSP meaning a Highly Sensitive Person. A highly sensitive person isn't to be confused with an attention seeker or overly sensitive people who enjoy unpleasant tantrum infused behaviors. It means you're high in sensory processing sensitivity. A pure HSP is usually very aware of the feelings of others and very reluctant to cause a scene.

So, as you may have guessed from the example I shared of your two friends, one of them does demonstrate empathy, which is excellent. But the other friend is more likely to be considered an empath.

A real empath goes beyond being an HSP; he or she also has empathic abilities which, when mastered, result in a very powerful being capable of various things such as healing others. But we'll get to tackle that a little later in the book.

The obvious question that follows is: how does one know whether they possess empathic abilities or not?

I mean, do you know if you're an empath? How about we finally shed some light on that.

A Self-diagnosis answering one question: Am I An Empath?

"I think we all have empathy. We may not have enough courage to display it."

-Maya Angelou

I grew up like most kids with parents who wanted me to fit in and be like all the other kids. Except I wasn't like the other kids. Being on my own made me feel better. I couldn't stand being in large crowds. Growing up, I remember watching something on television that was a particularly bad story, and it freaked me out. I don't recall precisely what the lousy story was about, but I do remember how shocked my mother was when 3 hours later she found me still locked up in my room sobbing hysterically.

These "incidents" kept showing up into my adult years, sometimes causing me to spend days in complete isolation, feeling very misunderstood by everyone, including my partner. For a while, I had a roommate, and I could feel their resentment and anger each time they walked through the door. It was almost like I was breathing in the energy of whoever was near me at any given point in time.

It was tough. People just called me moody, too sensitive and unpredictable. Growing up, I was told I needed to grow a thicker skin and stop taking everything so personally. But that's because no one in my environment took the time to understand what was happening inside me.

It's not easy going through daily life feeling like no one gets you. You know?

Truth be told, as I age and mature, it's becoming evident that there are various levels of being empathic. It's almost like a spectrum with varying degrees from the highest (true empaths with healing abilities) to those who are suffering from a serious deficiency (narcissists). Some people are highly sensitive and keenly aware of all the different energies around them, and there are those who've taken it to a whole new level where it's almost as though the surrounding energies of others overpower them. They feel in their bodies the same feeling, whether good or bad that another is experiencing.

These are the people who will often report this experience of other people's feelings becoming intrusive and uncontrollable. Regardless of how chronic your empathic levels are, it's prudent to do a self-assessment to be more mindful with who you're.

So here are reflective questions to help you in this quest to understand why you feel and experience life as you do. Keep in mind this list of questions is just an overview to help you get that initial clarity. If you would like to understand thyself deeper, then I recommend having a conversation with a coach or an empathy expert.

As a general rule of thumb, if you answer yes to at least 6 of these 12 questions, you're an empath with unusual gifts that need to be utilized positively in the world.

1. Am I usually drawn to animals and can sense their emotions?
2. Do I often feel overwhelmed in large crowds or the presence of others?
3. Am I powerfully drawn to people experiencing emotional pain?
4. Do I need to seclude myself from others regularly for some downtime?
5. Am I often dreaming vividly of future events and do my dreams usually come to pass?
6. Can I usually tell when someone isn't honest or authentic?
7. Do I possess any healing powers?
8. Does finding time for self-care often feel like a struggle for me?
9. Do I consider myself a free spirit with a distaste for control, rules, and routine?

10. Am I constantly struggling with my body weight?
11. Do I have an active, creative streak and a vivid imagination?
12. Is intense violence, the cruelty of any kind or tragedy utterly unbearable to me?

Congratulations!

Now you know more about who you're. If you answered yes to most if not all of the 12 questions, you not only have empathic abilities but you also have the opportunity to make a marked difference in our present world.

Yes, it's true. Empaths are having a particularly difficult time in our fast-paced modern world. There's a lot of negativity being broadcasted, and unfortunately, they come right at you. But be of good cheer, for all hope isn't lost. There is much work ahead of us if we want to turn things around and stop falling victim to the negative emotions being emanated.

This gift you have just discovered and validated is a blessing. But for you to harness and enjoy it as such, you'll need more awareness on how to groom yourself. So that you can walk around this earth as a positive force for good, healing those that require and request it, breathing into the atmosphere the nourishing energies that bring about prosperity, and playing your part as a loving, gifted being.

That is the new chapter of your life that awaits you, which is why I encourage to keep turning the pages of this book and discover how to elevate yourself to the point of thriving as an empath.

How does empathy show up, and what are the effects?

Most of the time, the things you might experience as you go through daily living may not make much sense to you and others around you, especially if you don't know you're an empath.

Often empaths feel like the weight of the world is on their shoulder. There's a tone of heaviness, sadness, anxiety, depression, and a general feeling of discomfort that's always looming in the background of everything they do.

I remember when I first landed my dream job working with a fast growing entertainment company that had establishments in America, Europe, and Africa. My friendships and family relationships were great, and I loved my job. It was the first time I was part of something so big and could afford to live in a big beautiful apartment in Jersey. To an outside observer, I had a perfect life.

But there was a discomfort I couldn't shake, and there was this heavy feeling constantly accompanying me. Most of my evenings were invested in attempts to deal with this enormous fatigue that even sleep wasn't curing. What was wrong?

Still unaware of my abilities, I didn't take cognizance of the various ways they were showing up in my daily life. So I kept bumping into conditions and circumstances that were creating very negative subtle sensations that impacted me.

Now your case might be different.

You could be experiencing discomfort more related to your health or relationships. Many people with empathic abilities report various health struggles and diseases such as agoraphobia, chronic fatigue, allergies, and fibromyalgia.

On an emotional level, the commonality that we see tends to be experiences of anxiety, depression, and even panic attacks. It could also be that you notice every time someone around you gets ill, you quickly pick up the same symptoms. Even simple things like regularly catching colds from others could be an effect of being a blind empath. You might also be getting a periodic blurred vision that you can't explain. Almost like there's a subtle, invisible layer preventing your eyes from seeing clearly.

And because we are usually so immersed in the feelings and stresses that others are experiencing, our self-care is often neglected because we forget to work on our exact inner needs since there are always layers from other people covering our real inner needs.

Other areas where you may need to observe to see what's showing up are:

Your relationships, love, and sexual experiences. If you find yourself recreating relationships that are toxic, unhealthy, and unproductive, this could be due to your empathic abilities that haven't yet been harnessed and controlled. We'll dive more into this in an upcoming chapter.

But here's something you need to remember. When you walk around unconsciously being controlled by your unique abilities, you'll often get sucked into partners and experiences that end up hurting you.

The tendency to overindulge or become addicted may also be an issue to watch out for. Empaths usually turn to addictions such as food, sex, drugs, alcohol, or even shopping to block out their sensitivities. Many struggles with weight issues because that extra padding is used as a defense mechanism to protect against negative energy.

Judith Orloff M.D and author of emotional freedom offer an energetic theory of obesity: "When empaths are thin, they've less insulation and are more vulnerable to absorbing stress. Early-twentieth-century faith healers were renowned for being grossly obese to avoid taking on their patients' symptoms, a common trap I've seen modern healing practitioners also unconsciously fall into; food is a grounding device." ("Judith Orloff M.D., The Energy of Food: A Missing Piece In Weight Loss'")

She also adds that many of her patients gain weight to protect against stress at home and work. Your perceptual abilities, vivid dreams, ability to sense people's energy, and a powerful intuition aren't to be ignored. These show up in your daily life because your high sensitivities can interpret and perceive things at a heightened level. The more you learn to harness your powers, the more empowered you'll become to use them in a positive, grounded way.

The effects you'll experience will very much vary

depending on how developed and nurtured your empathic abilities are. And what you'll notice is that the more you learn to appreciate and effectively utilize your gifts, the more joyous and liberated you'll feel.

Of course, there's a very positive and nourishing effect of being an empath. And they too will show up in your daily life. Learn to spot these and pour more attention on the positive special effects that you become aware of.

This can be an increased sense of creativity in the things you feel passionate about. It can also be your ability to be a great leader and team player. Yes, even if you're an introvert, you can still be a great leader because you're more inclined to notice the little details that others miss. Your ability to sense what others feel also makes you a significant asset at work because you'll deal with people fairly and with true understanding.

The particular resonance you oftentimes feel with nature, gardens, water or the bond you may feel with animal companions and people in need makes you a marvelous individual. It opens you up to the richness of nature and enables you to always see the bigger picture in life.

The list is never-ending, and the more you intentionally go into your day seeking out these positive effects, the longer your list becomes. So I encourage you to start making that list because contrary to what you were told growing up, empathic abilities aren't something to be ashamed of.

This is who you were born to be, and it's about time you unapologetically embrace the real you.

The false ideas you need to shed about being an Empath

There are so many myths and false concepts that have circulated over the years around being an empath, and I feel many of these ideas make it hard for us to live empowered lives. Let's start debunking a few of these and see if any of them hit a nerve for you.

False Idea #1: Being an empath is a spiritual thing

This is a fundamental misconception that segregates empaths. While the lines do sometimes cross over between science and spirituality, you don't need to be spiritual, religious, or a spiritual healer to be an empath.

In the book 'The Empath's Survival Guide' Judith

Orloff starts off saying that empaths have a hyperactive mirror neuron system so that we can sense what other people are going through, and that narcissists have empathy deficient disorder. That's a scientific fact, not spiritual speculation.

My Truth:

Scientific research has proven the existence of empaths. This is a very new study in the world of science, and we barely understand the neurology behind empathy in general. But new research is surfacing supporting the existence of empaths.

Dr. Michel Banissy, a Professor of Psychology at Goldsmiths, and his post-doctoral researcher, Dr. Natalie Bowling have spent years looking into empathy and mirror-touch synaesthesia. Though we still have a long way to go, findings are showing between one and two percent of the population does report experiencing conditions associated with being empathic.

And the fact still holds. My brain will demonstrate empathic abilities, whether I'm spiritually inclined or not. Therefore understanding empaths aren't supposed to be some esoteric wishy-washy impractical thing.

False Idea #2: Empathic abilities are a disorder or mental illness

While it's true that we frequently get hit with overwhelming situations and scenarios that leave us feeling physically sick, it's certainly not true that empaths suffer from mental disorders or anything of that kind.

My Truth:

The emotions and physical sensations you have aren't anything to be ashamed of. There isn't anything wrong with you! You aren't sick or crazy!

Let me say that again...

Don't be put to shame or feel less than because you possess abilities to perceive far greater things than the general public. The human population has become so desensitized it's easier to label and categorize those groups of people that don't fit into the model view of the status quo such as empath who possess powers of higher perception.

False Idea #3: Being an empath means you're weak and playing the victim

Emotions are for wimps and overly sensitive people. I bet you've heard that all your life. This false belief has been pervading human consciousness for centuries. Showing your emotions is often seen as a sign of weakness. A lot of people assume that empaths are weak powerless and co-dependent on others. Many believe empaths live in a state of victimhood always fearful of the world around them.

Revealing to people your truth and what you can sense in them is so scary for people that are disconnected from their own emotions, they often call you a freak. Perhaps this is why most empaths become recluse.

My Truth:

All these misconceptions are generalized biases and nothing close to the truth. The fact that we can quickly process emotions and sensations that the majority of the population doesn't understand doesn't mean we are weaker. If anything, we pay more attention to the feelings of others and spend a lot of attention to how we treat others. There's no need for you ever to justify or get offended when someone rejects who you're. Just remember for most people, your way of being is incomprehensible and illogical to their mind.

And when it comes to taking responsibility,

bouncing back from challenges and working hard to make a difference, empaths perform just as well as any other human being. An empath can be just as strong, responsible and thriving in the world as anyone else, so don't let other people's limitations or fears cause you to settle for anything less than what your heart desires.

False Idea #4: Empaths are all introverts.

It appears to be that the majority of empaths are introverts, but this is certainly not true across the board.

My Truth:

Individuals bearing all kinds of characteristics will possess empathic abilities. Don't feel like you have to "fit" into a particular category of anything to exercise your empathic gifts. You can be an extrovert, introvert, ambivert or none of the above and still be an empath.

The idea of introversion as a prerequisite for being an empath isn't accurate.

Now that you've shed some of the false notions that may have played a role in constricting, you take a moment to see if any other myths come up. I encourage you to write them down on a piece of paper and right next to them writes your truth. Convert all the current false beliefs in your mind about what it means to be an empath into constructive ideas that'll nourish a healthy mindset as you move on to the next chapter.

EMOTIONAL WELL-BEING AND HEALTH

"Health is your connection with your body."
- Unknown

Since we all know that being an empath is all about energy and our sensitivities, doesn't it make complete sense to be more proactive when it comes to managing the energies relating to our health and well-being?

Unfortunately, the information that's abundantly shared online is more focused on "hiding" and "protecting" myself from the world.

To me, there's a fundamental flaw in this mindset, because by only focusing on hiding myself or creating defensive strategies that keep the negative stuff out I'm essentially giving my power of attention and intention to the very thing I don't want.

Think about it for a minute. "Let me build a strong defense and shield for myself" can't be the only solution. It's good for immediate and temporary relief when faced with unexpected danger, but it can't be a long-term solution. It won't help me thrive or live a freedom based lifestyle because the activated vibration in this thought pattern is - I pick up negativity all the time.

Here's the thing.

When you're an empath, it's like being a sponge absorbing everything in your environment. But you don't have to be a walking human sponge or fall victim to this gift. You do have the power to be a highly sensitive person, but you can be capable of interpreting and sensing energy at a heightened level and still be the master controlling what enters your domain of authority and what's kept out.

Not only that, but you also have the power to enhance your abilities so that you emanate and "pick up vibrations" that are predominantly good for you. Did you know that?

Can you imagine how much better your world could become if you found this balance?

Your power becomes endless.

Deepak Chopra says understanding your unique mind-body type, or dosha, and learning how to make the right choices to reestablish balance is crucial if you want to enjoy excellent health. In an article responding to one of Oprah.com's followers where the question posed was by a 43-year-old woman who was experiencing anxiety and overwhelmed as she felt her world crumbling over, Chopra's response was straightforward and informative.

"In the system of conventional Indian medicine known as Ayurveda, one of the basic elements in a persons makeup is known as Vayu or wind. It gives rise to an attribute known as Vata, the aspect of the mind and body associated with spontaneity, change, resilience, and vitality. When Vata is out of balance, restlessness, worry, confusion, indecision, anxiety, and a general inability to settle down or see straight arise. ("Ask Deepak: How to attain balance when you're feeling overwhelmed, April 2010")

As you may have thought, most of us struggle with

many if not all of these symptoms, and it's not meant to be a healthy way of life for us. We need to eliminate the root of the problem and bring back that balance.

The key to doing that's to begin recognizing that you might have patterns of behavior that don't align with your true nature. The more you get into harmony with your power, find balance, and work on raising your energy, the easier it becomes to match yourself up with well-being and a healthy lifestyle. It starts with acquiring a new set of beliefs and a new perspective.

If you believe your powers make you weak and that you're at the mercy of everything and everyone in the world that'll be your dominant energy. And it's going to be tough creating any other reality.

What do you believe about your emotions and empathic abilities?

Understanding and controlling emotions

Modern society continues to do us a great disservice when it comes to an understanding and controlling our emotions even though science shows a direct correlation between great health and balanced emotions.

Because we've also inherited some debilitating patterns of thought, whenever there's conflict within, rather than taking the time to process the emotions, we often block them off and attempt to suck it up.

Thwarting emotions is very unhealthy both physically and mentally, especially for empaths who are always highly sensitive. So let's get back to basics with this topic.

What are feelings and emotions, and why do they matter?

Contrary to what most people think, feelings and emotions aren't the same.

An emotion is a chemical that gets released when we interpret a specific stimulus. A feeling is the integration of that released emotion, and we begin to become cognizant of the effects or consequence of the released emotion in our bodies and brain. Then a feedback loop gets created whereby that feeling causes more release of emotions, and our intensity of feeling increases in the process.

It's vital for us to have emotions because this is what helps us interpret the raw data about the world around us and our feelings to help us create meaning out of the data that we perceive. It goes without saying that for us as empaths, gaining mastery over the interpretation of the emotions we receive is vital. Equally as crucial is the fact that we need to increase emotional intelligence and develop filtering abilities so that as we process that highly sensitive psychological experience that's constantly taking place while we are exposed to other people, animals, and the environment. We need to hone in the ability to quickly "sort out" and identify the energies that we want to allow into our energetic space and those that we want to release as soon as possible to avoid getting hurt.

Most empaths want to know if they can choose only to feel good energies.

Well, you can. But the way you get to the level where you can discern and choose to interact and match up with only good energies predominantly depends on your emotional resilience.

Having the power of choice means you must be exposed to options from which you can pick and choose what you desire. So if you're looking to experience the best of the empathic experience, you need to stop running away from the negative (by running away you're giving it power over you) and instead grow into your power so that nothing you don't choose can take over your space. That requires diligence and practice. You need a lot of self-awareness, self-love, and self-understanding.

Your emotions are your guiding system. They help you navigate this human experience. How you feel at any given time is the conscious awareness of the frequency you're broadcasting to the universe, whether that emotion originated with you or not.

When your mind impedes the flow of emotions because they are either too overwhelming or conflicting, that affects your body and produces psychological distress and symptoms, which if left unchecked can turn into chronic physical and mental illness.

Emotional stress and blocked energies have been linked to mental illness and physical problems like digestive issues, back problems, heart disease, migraines, autoimmune disorders, insomnia, and so much more. The Journal of Psychiatry published a study they conducted in which they found that empaths are more susceptible to depression, and anxiety in general. The study concluded that socially anxious individuals might demonstrate a unique social cognitive abilities profile with high cognitive empathic tendencies and considerable accuracy in affective mental state attributions. It is this hyper-sensitivity to emotions that may also cause empaths to become ill more often than others when not adequately managed.

The more self-aware you become of your own emotions and better handle them, the easier it becomes to control and manage all the other emotions you pick up when interacting with the world. It's time to stop glossing over how you feel about yourself.

Do you feel safe in this world?

Do you feel misunderstood?

Do you feel alone and at the mercy of energies that are more powerful than you?

Your worth is beyond than you think, and you can control so much more than you realize.

Can you stop empathic abilities if you're tired of feeling emotionally drained and don't want that power anymore?

The short answer is, no. There's no stopping your gift. In this life, you don't get a choice over creation. As long as you're breathing and walking in that human body, you'll continue to co-create with life. The details and quality of that creation are entirely up to you, but you can't be able to stop or pause it.

All the gifts that you came to earth with are yours as long as you journey this human experience. You get to reckon how little or how much to use them. And they can become a burden or a blessing; even that's entirely up to you. Wanting to put an end to your ability to sense other people and the environment is a fight you can't win because, in the web of life, we are all connected. The only difference is some of us are more acutely aware of that connection than others.

What you would rather focus on is how to handle your emotions master your mind and better filter out the energies that you interact with as you go through your day. These are all things you can easily learn which will, in turn, help you better relate to the different sensations and energies around you constructively.

Learning to stop absorbing other people's symptoms

Soon after being introduced to the man that I thought would be my true soul mate, I've come into the realization that something wasn't right. Sure the intimacy felt incredible, and I was smitten, but I started noticing a pattern.

After spending a weekend with him, I would find myself on Sunday night curled up on my bed with the same flu he'd just caught. Oftentimes date night would be fun, but gosh it would drain the life out of me. I would justify the chronic fatigue and heaviness in various ways, but not once did I suspect I was absorbing his overly cynical and negative outlook on life and people. I felt like I was giving, giving, and giving some more, but he wasn't willing to give anything back.

Our dinner conversations spanned a variety of topics from politics to the current state of social media, much of which I was merely a silent listener trying to understand this man with whom I was deeply in love.

Unfortunately, as the weeks turned to months, my health, emotional stability, and overall well-being started taking a severe downturn.

Now, I'm not pointing fingers or blaming him for anything. I merely want to show you how sometimes the people closest to us can become catalysts to a lot of agonizing pain even without knowing it.

He wasn't necessarily a bad guy, and I'm sure for any other woman it wouldn't be an issue. But when you're an open sponge with a porous body that absorbs everything in your environment, the people you pay your most attention with can become a massive liability. This doesn't mean you become a lone wolf, far from it.

As I've learned over the years, it's more about learning to ground yourself and setting healthy boundaries that enable you to process emotions better and filter out the pain, stress, and conflicts that go on around you.

But first, you need to have the realization that this is happening in your life. You can't live in denial just because you care about someone.

Here's the most important thing to always remember:

When you realize there's a pattern in your life where certain people, situations, or triggers result in physical discomfort that can't be medically diagnosed, know that you're not imagining things or going crazy. You are simply a highly sensitive person with a gift that must be developed, nurtured, and successfully managed.

The whole purpose of learning to embrace your empathic abilities and becoming a true empath is so that you can stop being at the mercy of other people's pain, stresses, and conflicts.

Highly sensitive people absorb anything and everything, and oftentimes they've no control over it. A true empath has mastered his or her abilities and doesn't automatically get overwhelmed by the emotions of another. This is how I've personally redefined for myself what it means to be an empath. How are you going to redefine it for yourself?

If you're genuinely ready to gain mastery over your unique abilities, then it's time to equip yourself with simple living strategies that'll empower and help you center yourself so you can finally stop absorbing other people's dysfunctions.

1. Use the power of your breath.

First, you need to realize the power contained in your breathing. Whenever you suspect you're picking up someone else's symptoms, bring all your focused attention to your breath for a few minutes. Surrender to this simple act of breathing deeply in and out. Use it to ground yourself and connect to your power.

2. Name it to tame it.

Next, ask yourself - what's this emotional or physical distress I'm feeling? Whenever we put a label on something, we decrease the momentum of the impact, which gives us ample time to handle the'ssue constructively.

3. Evaluate it "at the moment."

Once you've brought it to the forefront of your mind, evaluate this emotion. Don't let this slide and take over your mind and body. Deal with it immediately before it grows into a monster.

Is the distress really yours or have you picked it up from something or someone? Sometimes the answer is both. If for example you're feeling deep fear and it's yours, gently confront what's causing it. And you can do this either on your own or by getting professional help. If however, you realize it'sn't yours, pinpoint the apparent generator and work on releasing it.

4. Take a step back.

This can be physically moving away so you can get

into a mindful space to handle the situation or it can be a mental movement. Either way, you want to be able to create some movement that allows you to start reaching for that sense of relief that's absolutely essential in releasing unwanted energies.

5. Become more aware of your mind-body connection.

Keep breathing deeply. Seek to find where in your body you feel most vulnerable. Chances are if you can see that spot where the alarm is going off you can quickly turn things around and step back into your power. The more you practice this exercise, the better you'll know how your body works.

For example, in my case, my solar plexus is where I go first because I know my tummy is always the first place my alarm hits. By the time I start feeling it on my left shoulder I know it's reached stage two, which means the'ssue is more serious and I need to do something fast.

The physical sensations may not be identical, but the same rule will be true for you. Our bodies are such beautiful communicators. We need to get better at understanding the signals they send.

So let's suppose for you it's a migraine headache or a

sore throat, the moment you become aware of these symptoms, sit in silence, relax your entire mind and body. Practice your deep breathing. Place the palm of your hand on the area and practice soothing yourself, giving yourself self-healing. Keep doing it and speaking with yourself until the discomfort dissipates. In the last chapter of this book, you'll find lots of other useful practices to test out.

If you've been battling with depression, panic attacks, or chronic pain for a long time, this simple method when done daily with intention will strengthen and comfort you. It's a great way to reconnect your mind and body and imbue yourself with that feeling of safety that we all need. No one can heal you better than you can heal yourself. Learn to trust that.

3

A QUICK WAY TO PROCESS PAIN

Pain is a huge topic for empaths, mainly because of most of the reports, stories, and information currently available present a very dull and gloomy world for an empath.

Dealing with pain head-on is no easy task, but it's crucial for us to learn how to become warriors when it comes to pain and suffering because of our health, longevity, and well-being depend on it.

I'm starting to think one of the main reasons empaths are often associated with constant depression, anxiety, and fatigue attacks is because they usually don't know how to deal with emotions of anger, pain, and suffering. Rather than handle them in healthy ways, they tend to absorb and suppress.

But did you know your emotions could be processed and metabolized the same way you process food? That's what I want to teach you right now.

Derived from the Greek word "em" (in) and "pathos" (feeling), the term empathic means you and I can "feel into" others' feelings. It means we are highly tuned in, sensitive, and capable of absorbing the energy being transmitted by the other. It makes us vulnerable to what science has termed as 'emotional contagion,' which means you'll absorb the emotions of whomever you interact with. The primary issue with that's we live in a world inundated with false ideas, negativity, and a lot of emotional torture. So pain and silent suffering is a vibration a lot of people are carrying around, and when exposed to it, whether we filter it out quickly or not, it still impacts us.

A large part of the anxiety, depression, and chronic pain that's so common among empaths belongs to the collective consciousness; the current stress, and suffering that humanity is undergoing. But most people have been conditioned into emotional illiteracy, and they've numbed themselves out from "feeling" their emotional broadcasts. But that doesn't mean they don't broadcast that energy anyways and you know what sucks? You and your heightened sensitivities will pick it up immediately upon encountering such a person. Then you'll be stuck with the burden of having to deal with that pain.

Do you know how to release pain and suffering from your energetic field in a healthy way?

I learned this lesson the hard way. There was a moment in my life when I was just a human sponge walking around absorbing sensations I didn't care for. It all felt entirely out of my control. I was always tired and in pain. Something was still aching in my body, and pain relievers became my perfect friends. It wasn't until I joined a Yoga class where my instructor, who took a very holistic approach to life, enlightened me on what was happening. My muscle tension, constant body aches, and continued migraine were all effects of accumulated pain that I was holding on to.

Whether it was my own or absorbed from another, that pain was causing significant issues in my functionality, but I didn't know it was possible to release it in healthy ways. Since I know empaths constantly have to deal with a lot of challenging energies, let me share the simple process I've been using ever since to release and clear off the pain and toxicity.

1. Take responsibility for the emotions you're experiencing. Whether or not the energy originated from you or someone else, it's in your energetic field now impacting your body, so take full responsibility for it.
2. Witness the emotions in your body. Feel your body with your eyes closed. Notice where it's and how it feels. Do your best to define it in present first tense and refrain from using words that victimize you. For example, rather than say, I feel hurt (a victim mentality that disempowers you) choose to say, I'm feeling hurting, or I'm angry, etc.
3. Now describe the thing or situation surrounding this feeling in the first person and how you're experiencing it.
4. Describe it in the second person as if you were an observer of that particular scenario.
5. Describe the same situation and feelings again, but this time in the third person as if you were a reporter writing for a magazine and notice how detached you now feel about the entire thing.

You may choose to carry out this exercise verbally or by writing it down on paper. If you prefer to write it down, be sure to make it ceremonial in the end by shredding it up into pieces or burning the paper and openly declare, "I release you and let you go. I now welcome universal divine love and fresh energy to fill my entire being. Do some mindful breathing, and once you "feel the shift" that's it! It is done. Now put on a song and dance in celebration or treat yourself to a cupcake (that would be me).

The key here is to notice how you feel at every stage of this process.

Pain and toxic emotions aren't states we need to be afraid of or get tormented by when we come across them. We need to know they are harmful to our health and well-being and learn to spot and release them quickly.

Unfortunately, there's a lot of pain and suffering floating around our planet. This is why it's so important to notice how you feel in your interaction with others. Learn to clean up your energy often and create rituals around your daily life that help you stay grounded as you interact with the world.

Influencing others emotionally:

The more you learn to become an empathic warrior always grounded in your true power, the easier it becomes for you to start positively influencing others emotionally.

Where there are pain and suffering, you can pour in joy and hope. Where there's anger, you can pour in affection and peace. Where there's any fear, you can cast it out with the energy of love that radiates from within you. If we are to heal our planet, it can only be as a result of learning to overcome our darkness and becoming so bright that our light starts to shine on others as well.

Your ability to sense and connect with the energy of another human being or animal doesn't just make you vulnerable; it also makes them vulnerable to whatever you're broadcasting. And if you're vibrational offering is higher and stronger in frequency, you can perform amazing miracles for people without them ever realizing what you've done. Think of the good you can do in the world once you master this.

CHAPTER 4: A FEW UNHEALTHY HABITS TO AVOID IF YOU'RE STRUGGLING WITH YOUR EMPATHIC ABILITIES

"Our bodies are our gardens – our wills are our gardeners."

-William Shakespeare

The struggle is real; no one can deny that. It is a challenging journey. Figuring out a healthy way to express yourself in the world, while simultaneously handling your emotions as well as the energies of those around you is no easy task and no one should ever make light of the path you're walking. It takes more than mere willpower to do it successfully.

I know how easy overwhelm and anxiety can creep up in my day, and I've seen my friends struggle to get a grip sometimes, which is why I always encourage empaths to stop being so hard on themselves when they do get stuck in a coping mechanism that'sn't helpful.

Unfortunately, most of the habits we tend to form only make things worse in the long run, and as a result, we end up intensifying the already challenging journey of being an empath in this world. I believe no one deserves to go through daily life feeling anxious, defeated, and at the mercy of coping mechanisms. So let me somehow enlighten some unhealthy things that I've seen fellow empaths struggling with in the hopes that you'll avoid these habits or eliminate them as soon as you spot them.

The aim here is to make you a strong, empowered empath and valuable member in your community, not a self-loathing "coping addict."

Marijuana and empaths

I know it's a common practice. Smoking weed does help numb out and dim down all the noise we constantly pick up. Many empaths feel way better with a daily dose no matter how small. But here's the thing. If you're smoking as a means to escape, the consequences of that decision can never be right.

It's a great temporary relief, but you know what? So is scrolling through your Facebook feed for an entire afternoon or binge-watching Netflix. Doesn't mean you should be doing it. As soon as you the euphoric effects subside, the same pain, angst, frustration will still be there. That temporary fix doesn't resolve anything. You want to have real solutions that change things for the better.

Earlier this month, one of my friends came to me with a very heartfelt confession. He's been trying to quit weed since the year began. That was his New Year's resolution because it had gotten to a point where it was a huge stress generator for him in that it was getting out of hand. He was somewhat addicted to doing it four times a day minimum. His first strategy was to lessen the dosage, and it seemed to work, but six months in, he was sitting on my couch, feeling helpless and freaked out.

"I mean I can manage to do it less. I'm down to just once or twice a day, but I feel like the more I emphasize it, the more it causes me to stress out which doesn't make me feel any better. I want to embrace my empathic abilities and learn to control and master my energy, and yes smoking weed does hinder my intuitive progress, which is why I'm so anxious to quit completely, but then the entire thing overwhelms me, and I end up clinging back to that daily dose. Am I just hopeless?"

If you've experienced something similar to marijuana or an addictive drug of whatever kind, my heart pours out to you. Trust that if you feel it's time to start a new chapter in your life, you'll have the strength and courage to free yourself from that addiction finally.

And maybe for you, it won't be such a massive battle like it's for my friend. Perhaps it'll just naturally phase itself out. However, if like him, you realize it's tougher than you anticipated, don't sit and suffer alone. Get professional help, join a community that can support you, and asks those you trust to help you build new rituals and triggers so you can slowly shed that old habit. You can't shame or force or punish yourself into new behavior; you must love yourself into it. Don't forget that.

Empaths and negative self-talk

Whenever something terrible happens, or you get into a fight (yes I know how much we hate confrontation), what's your natural impulse? Do you stoop low, feel a heavy burden come over you and wish you could curl up into a tiny ball and disappear? What about when someone suddenly gives you a huge compliment? Do you receive it or feel uncomfortable and unworthy of praise?

For most empaths, harsh arguments, negative situations, and unpleasant environments create a downward spiral that drops them right into the territory of self-loathing and self-judgment. It's always hard for us to spite or condemn other people, yet we do it all the time to ourselves.

Have you ever questioned why?

Negative self-talk is common in our population, and everyone seems to indulge in it more than we like to admit. Researchers estimate that we think on average about 50,000 – 70,000 thoughts each day and that about 80% are negative thoughts. That's a lot of negativity.

For us as empaths, this creates a serious problem. We have to be cautious of our negative thinking tendencies as well as avoid absorbing those of others. That's where the danger lies for us because if we're not careful, we can get affected in compelling ways by this pervading habit.

Blaming ourselves for things that we can't control

and putting ourselves down has got to stop. That's not to say you need to shift and become a Pollyanna. Forcing yourself into positive affirmations and positive thinking like the masses promote online is barely going to work for someone as sensitive as you.

I want you to become more self-aware. Practice being mindful of the mental temperature and the overall tone of your inner dialogue. Being more aware will serve you better than forcing yourself always to be a positive thinker. Realize that whatever your inner dialogue sounds like will become the most dominant energy or aura around you. If you discover it's mostly dull and cynical, don't stress over it for you'ren't stuck. You have the power to think a new thought, and as you think differently and change the way you handle yourself, life will reflect you the same positive change.

Start today creating new habits and inner conversations that are more in alignment with the aura you want to walk around in. As a highly sensitive being, the last thing you want is to use those powers to tear yourself down or poison yourself with self-manufactured negativity.

Emotional eating:

Yes, this too is a habit. As much as it may seem to be out of your control, you have the power to determine your relationship with food. Gobbling down mac and cheese or chocolate ice cream can make everything seem a little better... for a while. Overeating has this numbing effect that can help us soften the blow of unwanted energies, have you noticed?

But this can quickly escalate into an uncontrollable eating addiction that many empaths are known to fall into. Sure it can help you calm down and give you that instant distraction, a feeling of safety, security, and serenity that's often elusive. A tough, unbearable day can be soothed down quietly with some Netflix and chill with a big pint of ice cream or a dozen chocolate dementia cupcakes to help you stop feeling what you don't want to feel. But I want to encourage you to give up this coping mechanism because whether you realize it or not, this is a sign that you need to heal your relationship with food.

Emotional eating patterns are very much tied to the mental, emotional, physical, and even spiritual struggles we're dealing with. Besides, you can recall how sickly you feel afterward, right?

That's why it's so important to identify and recognize your triggers and create a strategy that'll help you better handle the situations that cause you to overeat. In an article published on August 15th, 2017 by Harvard Health publishing, they confirm that there are parts of the brain that are satisfied by eating high-fat or high-sugar foods. And of course, we know that any behavior that's rewarded will likely be repeated. That's why researchers and experts on this topic suggest distracting yourself even if it's just for five minutes. You need to come up with creative ways that interest you to help switch gears and pour your attention into something wildly different before that automatic impulse kicks in. It could be going out for a five-minute walk, putting on your favorite song and dancing as much as you can for those three minutes or whatever else resonates with you.

As someone who understands how tough it can be to change an old habit, mine being mostly that of constant negative self-talk, I want to ensure you get something more than just airy-fairy suggestions of how to handle yourself the next time a trigger hits that you know will lead you into an old habit. The last chapter of this book is reserved purely as a resource full of practical tips to help you thrive, and there's a sub-section with simple, healthy ways to soothe yourself into a calm grounded state whenever stressful situations and sensations arise. So be sure to read to the end.

Alcohol and empaths:

Did you know a lot of empaths turn to alcohol to "unwind" and take the edge off as a form of self-medication?

It's common for empaths who want to numb out overwhelm and the unwanted sensations they are experiencing to resort to consumption of alcohol. And the immediate effect is pretty good because one does feel somewhat relaxed. The only problem is, alcohol is highly addictive. According to American Addiction Center, because alcohol is a depressant and has a sedative effect, people often use the substance to unwind. As a person's BAC rises, they often experience increased levels of relaxation. (The connection between Anxiety and Alcohol November 2018)

Most of the time it does feel great to mask the underlying problems we're faced with and temporarily relieve ourselves of the suffocating effects that are often associated with being an empath, but when this starts to backfire (and trust me it'll) the consequences can be devastating.

I recently came across a blogger who is sharing how he's been drinking from the age of six to help get rid of the angst and discomfort that accompanied him whenever his parents dragged him into one of the many social gatherings. They are complete extroverts and always seemed to enjoy being in large crowds. It was a nightmare for him; they just thought he was "too emotional" and in the end, since he couldn't get out of it, his way of coping became sneaking in a drink or two. He called it "his miracle drug" because in just a few shots; he could quickly drive away from the depression, anxiety, paranoia, and overwhelm he was experiencing. It was his ticket to freedom.

But you and I both know this type of freedom is always very temporary. It took him 20 years of frequent alcohol intake (which eventually turned into a daily routine) to hit rock bottom and realize he's become his own worst nightmare. Alcohol worked until it didn't work anymore. And at 26yrs old, his body and mind refused to cooperate any longer. It was time to either make a change and save his life before it was too late or call it quits. I don't know how his journey is currently progressing, but with the support of online readers who are probably walking the same path, I'm sure he'll find a way to overcome the addiction.

The point for us to drill home is that alcoholism never ends well. Sure it gives that false sense of freedom and control, but what happens the next further down the road?

I know it has become a tool for survival for many empaths and sure, drinking is one way to improve your mood and escape anxiety for a time, but it's also the fastest way to imprison yourself, paralyze your future and bring about a lot of pain and grief to those closest to you.

Now I know what you're probably thinking...

Could a little alcohol be okay?

Surely one or two glasses a day isn't too bad. Well, that's still debatable. A new scientific study declares there's no safe level of drinking alcohol. The International Medical Journal, The Lancet, made headlines when they showed that in 2016, nearly 3 million deaths globally were correlated to alcohol use including 12% of deaths in males between the ages of 14- 49. (New scientific study: no safe level of alcohol in August 2018)

Whether or not you choose to make alcohol your "miracle medicine" is a choice only you can make. No one can tell you whether or not you can safely handle any amount of alcohol, because only you know how it feels once you ingest that first glass of wine or beer. Be conscious about your choice to drink alcohol and let that decision be based on how you want to show up in the world.

Procrastination:

Sometimes it gets hard to cope with everyday tasks as an empath, primarily when we haven't wholly owned our empathic abilities. To outsiders, you might seem like a lazy passive and spaced-out person, and I think that's one of the reasons why empaths struggle to transform this unhealthy habit. They often feel alone, misunderstood, and stuck with no one to come to their aid.

Procrastination doesn't just affect empaths. It is such a common habit even Ellen DeGeneres talked about it in her stand up comedy show. Procrastination is when we put off making a decision, or we avoid taking some form of action and usually for empaths, it's a coping mechanism.

Lynda Williams shares how procrastination has been a monster in her life, especially when dealing with depression. "It's easy to assume that people like me who procrastinate are lazy; the truth is, if I could do it now, I would," she says with tears rolling down her cheeks.

I think this is something we can all relate to at some level. And I've been caught in that awful cycle where I shame, and guilt myself, which only makes me feel worse and I still don't get done what I know needs to get done. I mean, even today, with all the knowledge, tools, and living strategies that I use to empower myself I still have to deal with procrastination from time to time.

Procrastination hits an all-time high for empaths when we are explicitly going through an evil spell. If there's too much overwhelm, anxiety or depression, it's a lot easier to procrastinate. I think it's because when our energy is low, it's just not possible to sell yourself into being productive and doing even something as silly as washing dishes. So you just let them sit there and pile up. And the more they pile up, the worse we feel which of course creates this cycle of doom and self-manufactured loathing.

Now before you stamp off this unhealthy habit as beyond our control (especially when we are going through tough times), it's important to remember that procrastination is rooted in fear.

When the energy of fear is tuned up within you whether that originated from you or someone else, your tendency to procrastinate is activated and soon after a feeling of guilt, shame, and self-remorse which then builds this new momentum. After a while, you won't even remember where this thing generated from and trying to force yourself out of that funk may not work. So rather than beating yourself up or forcing yourself to do something when you're not up to it, step back from the situation and permit yourself to be.

Take a nap if you have to and break that momentum first. Then remind yourself that fear is usually the energy culprit fueling this habit. So work on clearing your energy first and foremost before stepping back into the chores or goals you wish to accomplish.

EMBRACING THE EMPATH EXPERIENCE

"Before healing others, heal yourself."
-Gambian saying

This feels like an opportune time to dive a little deeper into the empath experience and what it feels like to go through life feeling everything.

I think it's important always to remember that every human being experiences varying degrees of empathy unless there's a particular discord within them that creates a block.

And life is chaotic for most, if not all, people. Finding peace and happiness isn't easy in our modern world, even for those who don't consider themselves empathic. Social media and news are great at amplifying the negative side of humanity, which only makes our interactions with others all the more challenging. What we must do is figure out the aspects that we have control over as we go through daily communications and work on enhancing them.

Therefore the empath experience isn't about making you feel like an alien from another planet. There's nothing wrong with how you experience this human journey. Just because people around you interact with life and interpret things at a different level from you doesn't make your high sensitivities good or bad. It just means your senses are refined. You are tuned in to the dance of life at an unprecedented level, and the best way to enjoy this dance is to figure out the best way you can make the most of it.

Living on a planet with eight Billion fellow humans is a bit crowded for an empath, but we are here for a reason. It's not an accident that you were given this gift and the best use of it would be in service to yourself and others.

While I know how tight public places, crowded malls, and large gatherings can be, I still believe it's possible to find the balance that enables you to interact with the world in ways that are comfortable and reassuring for you.

We know that as empaths walking into a room, a grocery store, a company meeting, a restaurant and even flying with other people can be a very overwhelming experience. I was recently on a short two hour flight, and because I hadn't slept my optimum eight hours sleep all week, my mind was a little bit hazy, and I was having a hard time controlling my energies as per usual. I sat down, buckled up, and rather than jump right into a book, I decided to observe what others around me were doing. It was a morning flight, my eyes were feeling the distress of sleeping so little, and I didn't feel like listening to music. So my attention landed on a group of rowdy young guys probably from Russia who were excited about being on a plane. The four of them caused quite a bit of ruckus coming in, and one of them had a tough time even paying attention to the instructions of the flight attendant. I couldn't tell if he was being stubborn or trying to flirt with her.

Either way, he was getting on her nerves, and I slowly started experiencing the same angst and irritation she was feeling. She also seemed to be enduring a sore throat, and the more I paid attention to this situation, the more I started feeling my throat tingle. I quickly caught myself absorbing the energy from the flight attendant and took the necessary precaution to filter it through. Having learned from past experiences where I would catch someone's anger or headache or some other symptom, I never let myself get too carried away even on my "hazy days." We can get overwhelmed and absorbed into different energies fast.

The vibes and emotional sensations being broadcasted from our surroundings are always real and vivid to us. It's no wonder we try to escape it all by any means necessary. Most of the time, the escape routes we choose end up hurting us far more, whether that be overeating, smoking, alcohol drug, or some other addiction.

I'm not here to make light of the daily struggle you face trying to fit into a society that'sn't very welcoming to our kind. I don't want you to fit into the status quo at all. That would destroy you.

What I do intend is for you to become proactive with your lifestyle choices and the framework for living that you establish.

If for example like my friend you've ended up abandoning a shopping cart in the middle of a supermarket because of how overwhelming things got during your Christmas shopping spree, rather than completely cut out shopping from your life, get more strategic with the timings when you choose to go shopping. Find out those times when crowds of people aren't storming in and enjoy doing your shopping in solace. You will still be exposed to the different energies of the staff, the few patrons who, like you, would instead shop in peaceful and quiet and you'll have more "breathing space" to interact with the energy of the food you purchase.

Public places don't need to be torturous if you create robust frameworks for living and a few tactics for engaging publicly at your own chosen time.

Some empaths find it unbearable to experience daily human living under normal social conditions, so they lock themselves away somewhere. They either move out of big cities into secluded farms or hardly ever leave their city apartment unless extremely necessary.

I can only base from firsthand experience when I say this. My conviction is that total isolation isn't the answer to happiness, peace of mind, and freedom for an empath. We indeed need solitude and frequent time alone but isolating ourselves as a result of fear or overwhelm means we end up settling for a very limited lifestyle. It is impossible to thrive when held captive to such limiting beliefs and emotions.

As we interact and respond to the world entirely in our power, I believe it becomes essential to master the art of only becoming aware of other people's energies and accepting them just as they are. In other words, I want you to train yourself to go out into the world, grounded in your own power, open to sensing emotions and vibes from others and rather than trying to fight them off or fix them, observe and filter them out. Those you wish to absorb remain with you and those that don't fit you flow back to their source.

I believe you have a choice to make as you continue reading this book. You can continue accepting a life of victimhood where even your own life doesn't feel like it's truly yours. Any interaction feels stressful because you're always anxious about taking in more than is right for you.

Or... You can choose to liberate yourself and your abilities.

There are many practical things you can do immediately, and I share some of these practical tips in the last chapter. I'll also be imparting with you some of the benefits of embracing the empathic experiences in an upcoming chapter because I want you to see all the good you can do once you fully own and master your powers. In so doing, you become an empowered empath who not only thrives but also heals the world in the process.

EMPATHS AND RELATIONSHIPS

"Empathy is the most precious human quality."
- Dalai Lama

Dealing with relationships as an empath is a big challenge. I'm sure you know what I mean. Whether it's professional, intimate, or family relationships, we love being deeply connected to others and sharing meaningful experiences but creating such relationships in our modern world is easier said than done.

We are highly creative, thoughtful, intuitive, super, passionate individuals, and the excitement we bring to any relationship when adequately understood is one to be savored. However, there are indeed lots of challenges to be faced as we attempt to create productive nourishing relationships that empower us. Majority of the people around us don't "feel" or process things as deeply as we do, and that can be very arduous to deal with.

So even though we too desire that chance to experience true love with a soul mate or nurture enriching relationships with the people we care about, our approach to love and all kinds of relationships needs to be somewhat unique given our highly sensitive nature. The struggle is real, and we've had to endure it for a long time. It's time to turn a new leaf.

Why you've been struggling with romance

Because we feel everything so intensely, being in love as an empath is out of this world. And I mean this in the positive and negative. When you find that right match, being madly in love and intensely passionate are a norm. The exchange of energy is incredible, and you tend to be very addicting for your partner. This can be a fantastic experience for both of you.

However, if you end up with a match that'sn't right for you, the same energetic exchange will have a substantial negative impact. This is probably why most empaths avoid intimacy. Once you've burned a few times from choosing poorly, your entire being refused to go down that dark path again.

The other issue is the fact that being moody often plays out when we get romantically involved. Because all our emotions are, such as joy, anger, sadness, or happiness are so heightened, sometimes they get out of control. What's worse is when you absorb the feelings of someone else while out and about with your partner that creates an entirely different outcome for the two of you.

Do you find yourself excited about starting a relationship only to feel burdened and freaked out a few months in?

This is mostly because, as empaths, we don't take the time to set healthy boundaries and fully express our sensitivities and dislikes to our new partner. If the person you're in a relationship with is right for you, they will understand and appreciate the fact that you regularly need space and alone time.

They won't impose their beliefs on you or compare your relationship with other people. The'ssue has never been your inability to be a good partner; it's about being romantically involved with someone who helps you emerge as the best version of yourself.

It's nearly impossible for us to hide our feelings and to be that vulnerable usually complicates things unless you have someone just like you or at least understands your nature. In our modern society where authenticity and genuine compassion, affection, and attention are a rare commodity, romance is a tough one for us. Superficial dating is the trend. We can't stand anything that'sn't authentic.

Showing off, trying to gather as much attention as possible, especially on social media is what "cool" couples do. That stuff turns us off.

How to handle intimate relationships as an empath

We all want to have meaningful relationships whether it's with a friend, a family member, co-worker, and especially those we fall madly in love with. Finding that special someone who is both your soul mate and best friend is no easy feat for empaths. The best way to cultivate and nurture an intimate relationship when you feel you've found the right person is by using your special abilities to form a healthy bond.

Notice I say a healthy bond.

Not just any bond. Your connection needs to run deep. Far more profound than the superficial level at which most people run their relationships. Because by default you're finely tuned to higher perceptions, you need to be with someone who can connect with you at that level too.

This is where science and spirituality crossfade into each other.

An intimate relationship that doesn't connect the two of you physically, mentally, emotionally, and spiritually will have a hard time lasting or satisfying you.

When I say spiritual connection, I'm not talking about a religious thing unless that's your preference. I mean you need to create a bond that's grounded in something more profound; it doesn't need to be religious or even spiritual (as defined by social norms). Depending on both your beliefs, it can be whatever grounds and empowers both of you.

In essence, what you want to do is create a container for being holistically connected and vulnerable with each other, where both of you pour in the best versions of yourselves until you develop this inner knowing that no matter what, your partner will be that empowering force for good in your life and vice-versa.

Couples with similar interests and viewpoints are better able to form this type of bond. It helps them develop habits and rituals that strengthen their bond and becomes a foundation for their relationship that can weather any storm.

As an empath, you know expressing your emotions come naturally, and when you're in love, it's almost magical. The best way to ensure these experiences turn into a lifetime of joy and meaningful experiences for you is by working on yourself so that you can easily match yourself up with someone worthy of enjoying this passionate ride of intimacy.

Settling for anything less than that special someone who lights you up is a big no-no. To help you with that, here are four tips for building a healthy intimate relationship and secure connection with your chosen partner.

1. Identify the primary intention of why you want to be in this relationship.

When you enter into a relationship with someone, don't do it blindly. Because the moment you start, it's as though the relationship becomes a third entity with its frequency. Have you noticed?

Most people don't even realize this. But being the highly sensitive person you're, you've probably had moments where you could tell there was third energy in the room.

Usually, after a few months of being together, it becomes more palpable since, in many instances, routine kicks in and momentum slows down. So you might even start to experience some heavy or dull energy that's neither yours nor your beloved's. This is because energy flows where attention goes. If one or both of you stop paying attention to the nurturing of your relationship, and instead life's obligations distract you, the energy of the relationships stagnates.

For an empath, this becomes a significant issue. Our less empathic counterparts would hardly pick up on this until things physically spiral out of control, but for us, we sense it immediately.

It's so important to get clear on why you're in the relationship in the first place. Go into it with clarity and powerful intentions. Discuss your plans with your partner, and make sure you're both on the same page.

2. Self-reflect as often as possible.

Whether you're looking to attract into your life someone special or have already entered into a relationship, nothing is more important than taking the time to find out who you're. The more you can continuously be in your body, present, fully aware, and grounded in your own power, the more enjoyable your intimate relationship becomes. That strong bond with another can only take place when you know who you're and what you desire.

Take a private journal now and jot down some thoughts to the following questions:

- What are your viewpoints on religion and spirituality?
- What does intimacy mean to you?
- How do you best like to express your love?
- How do you best like to receive love?
- How do you define romance?
- What are your core values?
- What are your viewpoints on religion and spirituality?

- What would you love to experience with your soulmate?
- What are some of your primary desires? Why do they matter to you, and how do you stay connected and real to them?
- Do you have daily rituals and practices that keep you grounded, such as meditation, prayer, devotion, etc.?
- Do you enjoy having higher consciousness conversations with someone you're in a relationship with? What about sexual explorations?

3. Prioritize meaningful conversations that openly express intimacy and affection.

Now that you've had some time to self-reflect and contemplate what matters to you, it's time to include the love of your life. Even if you're dating and it's not yet something serious, openly have this conversation with your beloved.

Share with them your viewpoints and give them the chance to open up as well and share where they stand. Finding out what's important to him or her right off the bat is a great way to start building that strong foundation and bond.

It also helps you realize sooner rather than later whether you two are traveling on the same path or if you're willing to step onto the same way together.

4. Give yourself space and downtime needed to manage your energy.

As you establish this open communication with your partner and they get to understand how special you're, one of the things you'll both need to agree on is creating that downtime and space necessary to help you reset regularly.

Aside from designing little practices that help you build a strong bond and express greater affection, giving you that solitude that every empath needs should be prioritized. If your partner is empathic as well, they too will benefit greatly from this agreement, but even if they aren't, I believe anyone who truly loves you'll understand and help you create a lifestyle that offers you greater joy and freedom.

Love is the most powerful force in our universe, and we know how to flow it passionately better than most. We must stop being afraid of freely offering our love and getting intimate with the right person. Of course, the caveat is "offering it to the right person."

So far, I've shared ways for you to be more open to intimacy and how to maintain a healthy relationship with the right partner. But we all know there are too many horrid stories of empaths who find themselves stuck in toxic relationships that feel like hell on earth. If you've been in such a relationship, you know how suffocating that can be. And it can certainly have very negative consequences, especially on your health. So before moving forward to the next chapter where we'll work on helping you thrive at work, let's touch on ways you can protect or free yourself from unhealthy relationships.

Protecting yourself from toxic relationships

Here are a few quickie tips to protect you from harmful relationships.

1. Re-evaluate your principles and core values:

The number one reason to enter into any relationship is that it makes you feel happier and brings out the best in you. Period. Which means your top values need to be aligned and activated within that relationship. So if for example, a core value is freedom, getting into a relationship with a control freak won't work no matter how smitten you're.

It's an excellent idea to sit and consciously make a

list of your core values and the principles by which to run your life. Then just underneath create another list of what I call "deal breakers." This is essentially a list of the qualities you most treasure in a partner and without these, you won't settle.

These are often qualities such as gentle, free-spirited, good listener, etc. Be sure though that this list is a reflection of the core values you possess and that you too are displaying the same qualities you seek in your partner. You can only attract what you're, not what you say you want.

2. Raise your personal standards:

Because empaths are so attractive and can get anyone (even total strangers) to open up and share their feelings, it can be tricky knowing when to pull the plug on a budding relationship.

Oftentimes it's just so easy to get into one we may not take the time to determine whether it's good for us consciously. That's why raising your standards is so vital. Your intimate relationships need to meet a particular criterion, which you determine. It can't just be anyone's game.

You are extremely valuable as a person. You're super passionate, gifted, and honestly, one of the best lovers anyone could have, so why just let anyone wiggle themselves into your private world? The higher you raise the bar when it comes to intimate relationships and close friendships, the harder it becomes for anything less than what you truly desire and deserve to push its way through into your world successfully.

3. Let the past go. Do you find that your history keeps sneaking up on you?

Like every time you date someone, you quickly realize they've the same negative traits that your parents had? If so, then you have what Freud called repetition compulsion. It could be a childhood condition that makes you feel like you deserve this "bad experience" because that's what you were raised with so in your mind it's "normal" for people to be condescending or mistreat you. But that's not true.

I'm here to make you realize that it's time to let go of your past. You aren't your past failures or your parent's limitations. How others have treated you or reacted to you in the past hasn'thing to do with who you're, and it's about time to release the old and embrace a new you.

5. Work on your sense of deservability.

Have you spent your whole life struggling with feelings of unworthiness? Do you often have voices in your head, asking, "Who are you to be loved deeply?"

It's very challenging to live a fulfilled life and find someone who will love you for all that you're when you silently doubt how much you deserve it. I know your background, society, and experience may have created lots of tension in your mind about what you deserve to experience in this life, but I strongly urge you to question those beliefs. You need to know and believe that you deserve a good life, a safe space to live and work. And you must understand that you deserve to be loved because you're loveable.

The more confident and deserving you feel about being loved by someone beautiful, the easier it'll be to only match up with a partner that'll enhance your life. It's effortless really, what you believe you deserve is what you'll attract from others, so work on this as much as possible.

6. Practice self-love.

Sure, you've seen and heard this concept everywhere online. But do you practice it? If you're always keenly aware of how awful your body, career or sensitivities are, it's highly unlikely you'll find anyone who can truly love you.

Most of us are so giving and loving to others, yet we can barely look at ourselves straight in the mirror after a shower without feeling shame disgust or self-loathing.

To be loveable, you must first love yourself. Love is all around you, but for you to experience more of it, you must be giving from a place of wholeness and self-acceptance.

7. Set clear intentions and a positive, energetic shield around yourself.

I'm not entirely convinced that building protective shields leads to a happier, prosperous life for empaths. But what I certainly know is that we work with energy. As such, we can be more intentional about the dominant energy that we emanate at any given moment. If you train yourself to be expansive and strongly concentrated with passionate, powerful, and highly positive energy, by the universal law of cause and effect, you can only produce results that correspond to that cause.

So rather than worry too much about building protective shields that keep toxic people out, focus on becoming a source of powerful positive energy that encapsulates your entire being as you go through daily human interactions and watch how different things become for you.

As an empath, you have special needs, and it's important to honor yours and communicate them to the people you're in a relationship with. There are many wonderful strategies and practical tips that you'll be getting at the end of the book to equip you with the solutions that'll lead to a thriving holistic lifestyle. Now you feel a little more equipped to deal with all kinds of relationships, don't you? Let's keep going.

EMPATHS AND WORK

"My feeling is we need more compassion, we need more empathy, and we need more togetherness, in terms of working together."

- Cindy McCain

According to Harvard Health Publishing, there's an overlooked issue in the workplace where employees are silently struggling with some form of mental illness, yet no one wants to address it.

"Researchers analyzing results from the U.S National Comorbidity Survey, a nationally representative study of Americans ages 15 to 54 reported that 18% of those who were employed said they experience symptoms of a mental disorder in the previous month."("Mental health problems in the workplace, February 2010")

A similar survey was done by mental health charity, mind in the U.K where more than 44,000employees were surveyed and 48% of all people who participated said they experienced a mental health problem in their current job. And of that 48 %, only half of those people struggling with this experience ever talked to their employer about it. So basically we are looking at one in four U.K workers silently struggling in the workplace. I bet if we check in other countries as well, we'll find a lot of people who are going to work every morning and hating every minute of it.

Are you currently experiencing a similar issue? Are you feeling so drained, burnt out, and misunderstood in the workplace that quitting seems like the only option? Or perhaps you've previously left in frustration only to land another job or start a new business that later on became burdensome. Because you're an empath, the work experience will require you to approach things differently if you want to thrive and live well.

I know many empaths are told they need to take up

jobs that are more intuitive, spiritual, and healing in nature such as therapy or other "helping" professions, but here's the thing. The main reason work becomes a struggle, and at times, a nightmare is because of the energy battles and emotional conflicts you keep facing.

Meaning, it's all about your energy and how you're protecting it. If you're absorbing so much negative energy in your environment and succumbing to its ill effects, switching to a different job, career or business may not be the best answer. So before giving up hope about your current work situation and feeling doomed, let's review some key insights that I think will help protect and nourish your empathic abilities in the workplace.

How to approach your work and career

It's straightforward. Your heart must be in line with the work that you do to thrive as an empath. Forget about what loud-mouthed motivators, marketers, and cynics of this world say. This is the best time in human history to be alive. You know why?

You can control your own destiny.

Never has it been more feasible and easier for anyone, anywhere to create the quality of life they desire. It doesn't matter what your vocation is, as long as you build a strong foundation around it, you'll succeed.

The way you approach your work or job, as an empath ought to be the same way you approach everything else in life. You and I both know compartmentalizing doesn't work for empaths. Why put yourself through the trauma that comes from trying to settle for work that doesn't align with your core values and sensitivities?

Remember the exercise we did for attracting better relationships? I encourage you to do the same for your work. Approach it like you would meeting a soul mate and make a list of all the qualities, experiences, and criterion you wish your work life to embody. It doesn't matter whether you're an entrepreneur serving clients or an employee with a boss, colleagues, and clients to think of. It is the intention you set and the grounding foundations you establish that'll determine how much you can enjoy your work-life.

Generally, empaths are drawn to mission-driven, meaningful work that makes a difference in the world. Because you know this to be true of you, do everything you can to align with opportunities that reflect this truth.

However, don't fall for the misconception that it means you must become a spiritual healer, psychic medium, coach, or any of the various helping professions associated with empathic abilities.

I know empaths who are engineers, managers, entrepreneurs, doctors, and even investment bankers. There is no limit to the contribution you can make to the world with your gifts, and you need never limit yourself to thinking that only artists and healers get to build careers using their empathic abilities. If anything, I believe the more you become empowered as an empath, the more helpful you'll be in areas like HR and senior management positions where people are feeling unappreciated. But you can't help or give if you're still overwhelmed, uncontrolled, and unstable in your power. As that Gambian saying reveals, we must first heal ourselves before extending out to help others.

You need to gain full understanding and control of your sensitivities and use it in powerfully positive ways.

The more you understand energy and the way it

works, the easier it'll be to make smart choices on your job role.

Contrary to common belief, you don't have to choose between making money and helping people. And you certainly don't have to pretend to be something you're not just to fit into a work environment. When you compromise who you're, you can never do your best work. So rather than approaching your work from the viewpoint of "trying to fit in," I invite you to figure out what your strengths are, the contribution you want to make to our global economy and the gifts and skills you want to develop that align with your empathic powers. From there, choose the vocation that best ticks all those boxes.

Lynn Taylor, a national workplace exper and author of Tame Your Terrible Office Tyrant; How to Manage Childish Boss Behavior and Thrive in Your Job says, "people want to connect on a humane level in the office; the alternative is a sterile environment with low productivity. So, the more you demonstrate these abilities, the faster your career will advance. It's the 'office diplomats' with keen emotional intelligence who are most likely to be influential, effective corporate leaders. They realize those trusting relationships built on diplomacy and respect are at the heart of both individual success and organizational productivity. An ounce of people sensitivity is worth a pound of cure when it comes to daily human interaction and mitigating conflict. By developing these skills, you'll reduce bad behavior in the office, and your positive approach will be contagious."

An ounce of your sensitivities is worth a pound of cure in today's business world.

This to me, is the free pass empaths have been waiting for. It's the confirmation that the workplace is shifting in a significant way. Business is getting a makeover. Authenticity is now one of the crucial things customers demand. Empowerment, empathy, and genuine connection are what every employee craves. And everyone now recognizes that empowered empaths are valuable members of the workplace. Your time to flourish as an empowered empath has come provided you do the groundwork within yourself.

Feeling safe and empowered at work.

Chances are, the more you feel empowered, valued and appreciated for your abilities, the more satisfied and fulfilled you'll be with your chosen vocation. I'm permitting you right here and now to stop exhausting yourself and applying strenuous effort to fit into a work environment that doesn't suit you.

By now, you're well aware that when certain things are in your immediate working environment, you don't perform at your best. Anxiety jumps in and takes over very quickly for empaths, so we need to make sure you set parameters that help reduce or eliminate anxiety triggers.

One: Excessive sounds, lights, or continuous interpersonal interaction from co-workers can become a drain for us and cause us to feel exhausted.

Helpful hint:

Consider taking a personal initiative to create a safe environment for yourself around the workplace. For example, if you have to work in a place with lots of noise and there's no possible option to get moved somewhere quiet, invest in a headset piece that cuts out all noise.

What are some other small creative things you can do to improve your immediate work environment?

Two: Decluttering your workspace and always

ensuring it's clean is super important. And you can't leave it to the company to take care of it whether they pay a great cleaning team or not.

The decorations, sense of ease, and organization around your desk are your responsibility, and it does affect you because your energy is immersed in that state for several hours each day.

Many empaths and highly sensitive people report feeling unsettled in cluttered environments. There's too much sensory information to process.

Helpful Hint:

Consider going for a minimalist set up in your work environment. Declutter your office or workspace regularly and create a sensation of relaxation, openness, and calmness as much as you can.

Three: Work on simplifying that complex inner dialogue that makes you feel it's not okay to be sensitive and cognizant of other people's emotions at work.

As you have learned thus far, not only is it a beautiful thing that you possess empathic abilities, even the workplace is slowly shifting to the understanding that leaders with your qualities might be the best way forward. This means the more you can tame your wild inner dialogue and shift your old beliefs to perceiving yourself as a powerful, valued force for good, the easier it'll be for others to receive that broadcast and reflect it back to you.

Helpful Hint:

Regardless of where you work or travel to in this world, a real feeling of safety, peace, and empowerment can only be born from within. There will never be someone from the outside who comes and solves your issues. You are the only one who can train your mind into positive, constructive thinking. Learn to perceive yourself as reliable, powerful, safe, and secure.

To seek security from the outside world is a temporary solution that'll keep backfiring on you. So what do you think it'll require for you to develop an inner dialogue of safety, security, and empowerment today?

Four: Trying to please everyone or going out of your way to avoid conflict even if it means absorbing and holding on to that negative energy will never be a good long-term strategy if you want to thrive as an empath.

I mean think about it, whether you're employed, a freelancer or a business owner you'll always be dealing with people. And there are good and bad people no matter where you look. You could just as easily find a boss or customer that's tough to deal with.

Helpful Hint:

Establish a healthier way (that resonates with your personality) to deal with such situations. Using verbal Aikido, for example, might be a great option to consider.

Five: Aggression in the workplace is often acceptable for our less empathic counterparts, but we know how harmful it can be for us. It's essential you never allow your energy to get sucked into the whirlpool that aggressive colleagues and even customers enjoy because, to me, those who are always stirring up arguments, tantrums and verbally attacking others are merely projecting their insecurities. Don't fall into that trap.

Helpful Hint:

Ever heard of verbal Aikido? This is the perfect time to practice it. Aikido is a modern Japanese martial art created by a martial arts master named Morihei

Ueshiba. The fundamental principle underlying this martial arts is that during any conflict, we should always seek to neutralize, not harm, the opponent.

In practicing this, we would be applying the underlying philosophy of personal evolution in the context of dealing with the verbal and energetic exchange. It would require us to integrate all our sensitivities and practice mental, emotional, and spiritual self-control to our communication. I'm not saying it's easy to do or that you'll get it right the first time, but if you're tired of running, hiding and absorbing conflict like a powerless victim, it's worth a try. Like any technique, the more you learn and practice it, the higher the benefits.

Finding work that works for you

Now that you're beginning to see that the working world isn't meant to be a hostile torturous place for you, how about we figure out what work will give you that sense of fulfillment and satisfaction.

As Einstein once said, the most important question you can ever ask yourself is, Is this a friendly universe? If your answer is yes, then surely this universe wants you to enjoy full expression of your skills and natural gifts in every way possible, including your work life. I believe we are all here for something meaningful, and we have to find out what we can be and do on planet earth that brings meaning to others and ourselves. If this is how you view your work life, you can't go wrong. The question is, where do you begin?

Make the most of your sensitivities.

Rather than treating your empathic abilities as some mistake that makes you a misfit in society, think of them as the superpowers that make you instantly unique. In truth, I believe that's precisely what they are.

That doesn't mean you're better or more special than other individuals; it just means these are the gifts you were given to explore, work with and eventually utilize for the highest good of all people.

Judith Orloff M.D also believes that as an empath, we can only excel and enjoy our work when we express our intuition, thoughtfulness, quietness, and creativity. She presents the pros and cons of individual careers and working conditions based on her experience and feels that empaths do better in lower stress environments, solo jobs, or with small companies. She also says that many of her patients prefer being self-employed to avoid drain and overwhelm from co-workers, bosses, and packed schedules. But here's the thing. It's not a standard rule. As I mentioned before, I know empaths that are engineers and doctors running a tight schedule and receiving fantastic recognition for their work.

So giving you a linear answer to such a complex topic that's purely relative to the individual wouldn't be fair to your growth and progress. What I can tell you is this. You don't have to be a writer, health care professional, musician, graphics designer, animal rescuer, psychotherapist, or a life coach to thrive as an empath. If you're not doing work that enables you to demonstrate the highest expression of your most authentic Self, even a seemingly empathic profession like healing others can drain and overwhelm you.

I've a Spanish friend who used to be a card reader and energy healer. But she was always sick, felt lonely, and could never make enough money to pay her monthly bills. We first met at a Starbucks coffee shop where I was sitting busily typing on my computer, and she was frantically moving up and down in search of a power plug to charge her dying phone.

When I noticed she was struggling to get anyone to

share with her their spot, I offered up mine and asked her to sit and join me while her phone recharged. That became the beginning of a very heartfelt conversation where I learned all about her struggles and gifts. I quickly realized she was an empath. She had never heard of this term, but it made complete sense to her. After hearing how unhappy she was despite the joy she felt when someone got healed during her treatments, I encouraged her to contemplate her underlying beliefs. What she needed was a paradigm shift. The same paradigm shift you'll be experiencing in the next chapter. Six months after we became friends, she was working in a retirement home fulltime, and her health had greatly improved. Now she's working on tapping into that right frequency of a loving soul mate, and you know what? I don't doubt in my mind she's just about to bump into him.

I've come across many life coaches, therapists, and healers who need more help than the patients they are trying to heal. And I've also come across life coaches and energy healers with profitable businesses.

Bottom line?

The work that enables you to express the best and

highest version of yourself while integrating your empathic abilities is the only work you should be going after. Your skills, temperament, and gifts are valuable to all kinds of careers. So use your intuition when considering a job or business to go into. Make sure in your gut and your body it feels right and that you resonate with space, people, energy and environment you want to serve.

This is by far the best way to take care of your energy and enhance your empathic abilities. It will also reduce the risk of always being drained and fatigued at work. Here's just a short list of jobs experts on this topic recommend you avoid and those they suggest you consider. If none of them feels right, do a little more research online based on your skills, talent, and passion and choose to bet on yourself.

Jobs to avoid:

- Politics.
- Attorney.
- Executive manager for large corporations.
- Used car salesman.
- A cashier at big store chains.
- Policeman or Policewoman.

- Fire fighter.
- Public relations.

Jobs to consider:

- Veterinary.
- Massage therapist.
- Working at an animal shelter or animal rescue.
- An employee at a non-profit organization.
- Hospice worker.
- Social worker.
- Psychotherapist.

Chinese medical practitioners.

THE GIFT OF BEING AN EMPATH

"The higher your energy level, the more efficient your body. The more efficient your body, the better you feel, and the more you'll use your talent to produce outstanding results."

- Tony Robbins.

At this point in our journey together, it must be clear to you that I'm a strong advocate for owning your empathic abilities and proudly showing them to the world.

Yes, there's the challenge that comes with that given how rigid and impervious our society has become. A significant portion of our global population sits on the middle to the extreme opposite end spectrum of the empathy scale, where they've made it seem like it's reasonable to "feel nothing." So on those times when it feels hard embracing your unique abilities, step back from the heat of the moment and ground yourself in the truth.

What truth?

This is a journey, and you'll go through different stages that'll move you from that state of feeling burdened by your gifts to feeling fully empowered. Often you'll come into contact with people who are also going through their tests, trials, and tribulations and depending on their level of awareness, they may or may not appreciate you for who you're. There's nothing wrong with that; learn to see the value in everyone's point of view without compromising yours.

You are a unique individual; a piece of life itself made to perfection. Everything you possess is there not by accident, but by design, including your empathic abilities. On the empathy spectrum, you sit high up on that scale where it's not just about being a highly sensitive person; it's about being a gifted person who can perceive and interpret life with incredible detail.

This is an excellent thing. Your heightened level of awareness must never be shut down, muted off or hidden from the world. You need a constant reminder telling you that you're a valuable member of our society - you're more than good enough. The beautiful traits you possess set you apart and give you the advantage you need to design your dream lifestyle.

Take a deep breath in, repeat that sentence if you need to and soak in it for a moment.

I'm a valuable member of my community. I'm more than good enough and where I'm now is the right place and the right time for me to start shining.

Receive this knowing and live from it starting now.

The paradigm shift that gives you the freedom to be an empath.

Let me set the stage here by warning you that you may not fully agree with this section of the book and that's okay. However, don't back out from reading it with an open mind and heart as you never know what may come of it.

Most of the information we have on the Internet around empaths, the struggle of dealing with the world and the dangers of falling for narcissists and energy vampires tend to be very one-sided. There is a tendency to make it seem as though it's out of our control as empaths. What we fail to discuss openly is the fact that there are underlying beliefs that shape all our realities. When those beliefs are detrimental to our wellbeing, it becomes a self-fulfilling prophecy whereby we produce conditions, situations, and experiences corresponding to said expectations.

For us to grow as human beings and especially as empaths, we must gather enough courage and confront the lies that we often tell ourselves.

What we find in the world is a reflection of our underlying paradigms.

Yes, this is a tough one to swallow, but it's true nonetheless. The tendency to get into relationships or situations that make you a pathological giver is rooted in a negative belief system active within you.

Your willingness to self-sacrifice, the insecurities, self-doubt, and other negative thought patterns are what make you perfect prey for narcissists and other energy vampires. So one of the dominant paradigm shifts you need to address boldly is the active belief that your needs are illegitimate, less worthy and that you're undeserving of having the best in life.

Because of your highly sensitive nature and depending on your upbringing, you could be running on a belief system that was conditioned during your formative years to perceive yourself as a burden and someone weak and too passive. If that's the case, then emotions like resentment, anger, pain even loneliness could be buried deep within and project themselves in your life in the most unusual ways.

Let me give you another example of my Spanish friend. She had been married once to a man she could only describe as a sadistic control freak. He not only mistreated her during their marriage but also made sure he left her feeling worthless and undeserving of ever being loved the day he ran off with another woman.

When she started working on herself and the story of her former husband came up, she was still emotionally tormented by the entire experience. It was as if he was still alive in her controlling her emotions.

She felt small and insignificant. Her entire energy

would shift as soon as she started talking about him. She wanted to remarry and fall in love, of course, but the truth is, she was better off being on her own until she figured out the limiting beliefs that ruled her mind. Working on herself and building a new paradigm was the prudent thing to do before attempting to call in another relationship.

The mere fact that three years after he left she was still feeling like the betrayed victim full of resentment, hurt and anger for having given him too much was precisely why I told her to work on shifting her paradigm first. The'ssue isn't who was right or wrong. Here is a classic case of an empath that never realizes the underlying belief system that causes such conditions to manifest in her life. I want you to free yourself from that same trap if you recognize a pattern with your current work or relationships.

Victim mentality is a very twisted and complex belief system to possess and will require some effort from your end to even become aware of what's going on underneath. Because you have access to the emotions of everyone around you, it's all too easy to get yourself entangled and completely lose access to the depth of your own beliefs. That's why your freedom begins with becoming aware of the long-held belief system and shifting it accordingly.

Take a chance now to be mindful of what you believe about yourself. And I don't mean the surface level affirmations or things you say to others. See yourself in the mirror and go as deep as you can.

Taking back your power

Most of what messes you up and keeps you from being your best self are underlying beliefs from childhood that just don't fit into a healthy, prosperous adult lifestyle.

You need to be courage and boldness. Face your own darkened energies and start healing those aspects of you that demonstrate these underlying negative beliefs. Your state of consciousness, and the beliefs you hold are projected outwardly in the people you meet, the quality of life you have and the happiness your experience. Therefore taking your power back is a matter of learning how to retrain your mind and getting more control over your energies so that you can establish new parameters and belief systems which will ultimately alter the conditions of your life.

As Nicolas Tesla once said, if you want to find the

secrets of the universe, think in terms of energy, frequency, and vibration. Your power lies in your ability to control the energy, frequency, and vibration you're predominantly in. If fundamentally you got trained into a lower frequency and negative thought patterns, it'll feel like an uphill climb where you're barely surviving. But once you understand how to use your empathic abilities to retrain your mind and build a new set of beliefs that support a high-quality life, accessing the energy, frequency, and vibration that heals, nourishes and prospers your life and others will become a new norm for you.

Nothing and no one has the superior ability over you; except the power you grant them.

Going beyond survival so you can thrive

Anyone can help you survive and in fact, most of the information available today is about showing you how to avoid things that overwhelm or scare you. In other words, about helping you cope and survive. But a life where you're just striving to survive and keep your head above water isn't really meaningful life. Wouldn't you agree?

You deserve to live a life you can't wait to unwrap.

And the only way to go beyond survival mode into thriving is by increasing your sense of personal responsibility. You've got to do your part and stop waiting for something or someone to come and give you the breakthrough or transformation you need.

Success and happiness come as you keep on keeping on, and it's always a forward and upward movement. That means you need to align yourself with inspired action and always focus on the little steps you can take right where you stand, to feel more in control of your energy, your life, and your destiny.

The worst part about being an empath is fighting to reclaim that sense of power. It does require massive effort to win that battle, but in the end, it's always worth it.

The best part is realizing that you can reclaim and restore yourself into a life far greater than your wildest imagination. It begins with a single choice to move forward and upward. It's time for you to make that choice and reach for your breakthrough. You are meant to be an example that others can emulate, and as the world shifts in consciousness to more self-awareness, we sure could use more of your true self.

So what do you say? Are you ready to start living from a place of power and complete self-acceptance?

Now, do you recall in an earlier chapter I alluded to the fact that being an empath and embracing this experience comes with some amazing advantages? Benefits that make you a powerful, valuable individual on this planet and quite frankly, it increases the "fun factor" of possessing some of your unique abilities.

Here's what I mean:

The gift of being an empath, and yes, it's a gift that can be used practically in your daily life to benefit those you love and yourself.

Your nurturing energy helps the planet, and all creatures flourish.

Regardless of what's happening globally, your ability to connect deeply with energy means you can nurture and pour nourishing, vitalizing energy into animals, people, places, and the entire planet.

Your creativity can beautify the world, solve problems, and add value to the global marketplace.

We are naturally very intuitive and creative as

empaths, and this can be utilized far beyond artistic fields. Because we think differently, innovation and creativity come more naturally to us, and as you might have guessed, the business world of today is all about innovation and creativity. So don't be shy, put your creativity on overdrive and share it with the world as you see fit. Find the thing that absorbs you and makes you come alive and allow it to turn into a creative out-put remaining detached from the outcome. It might end up being a hobby or something that makes you a fortune. Either way, permit yourself to share your creativity with the world.

You can support and help build greater collaborations, connections, and leadership structures.

Bet you never expected to hear that!

As the global marketplace shifts, a new group of leaders is emerging. People recognize that to be an effective leader; one must be sensitive and skilled enough to understand other people's feelings. An article posted on the Financial Post said, "If corporations want to attain greater levels of ethics, work on their capacity to be empathic should be their first move. ("Forget ethics training: focus on empathy, June 21, 2013")

Your ability to sense, understand, and deeply connected with people makes you a peacemaker and a valuable asset in the workplace assuming you have already grounded and worked on yourself as discussed in previous chapters. Your empathic abilities will enable you to notice the details that others miss, acknowledge other's needs, and motivate people to contribute their best efforts.

The world and the marketplace cry out for more empathy, and no one demonstrates empathy better than an empath.

Your strong intuition can help save lives and avoid wrong, dangerous, or poor choices.

Because your intuition is so highly developed, you can always rely on that gut feeling or hunch which will never lead you astray. This can be super valuable when you or a loved one is faced with a tough or confusing choice to make. You always have that inner knowing when something feels "off" or when it's "just right," and you can use this ability to help others in everyday life.

You get to be a constant authentic real human being that others can always rely on.

In a world where everyone's struggling to be

someone else and constantly seeks to outshine, outperform and compete with others, most human beings are wearing masks and hardly know their truth from what so-called gurus have fed them. Most people are imprisoned by their egos, trying to be trendy and you by default are the exact opposite. Your high sensitivity, vulnerability, and empathic abilities make you authentic, real, and more willing to speak your truth. You naturally engage your heart and mind in everything you do, and that has become a rare commodity in our modern society. You can be yourself and demonstrate by example to others what authenticity looks and feels like. It's always so refreshing to have a friend, who is still real, always speaks from their heart and always shows up as their real self. You can be that friend and role model.

EMPATHS, SPIRITUALITY, AND PSYCHIC ABILITIES

Life is like a tree, and its root is consciousness. Therefore, once we tend the root, the tree as a whole will be healthy.

-Deepak Chopra

Although some people have a strong disdain for spirituality in the context of being empathic, this book would be incomplete and to some extent unjust if we completely disregard the connection between spirituality and the empathic experience.

Does spirituality conflict with being an empath?

The simple answer is no.

Whether you actively subscribe to a spiritually conscious life or not, you can enjoy being an empath and use your gifts in positive ways, yet the underlying truth will remain unaltered for, in reality, spirituality is never in conflict with anything. Self-awareness, intuition, healing, connection are all essential for an empath, and yet they very much fall into the field of spirituality.

Carl Sagan, a world-renowned scientist, was quoted saying that science isn't only compatible with spirituality; it's a profound source of spirituality. His statement is worth pondering over for a while as it carries great significance for us as empaths.

The need to segregate and separate things in our world has caused some of the worst conflicts to arise. This gift of being an empath is meant to be used as a force for good in this world, and unless you find a way to be more integrative in your thought process when it comes to your world views, it's going to be tough feeling fully empowered in life.

Life is only one. Unity is the core of life itself, which means trying to make your powers either non-spiritual or only spiritual is still walking out of harmony with the fundamental laws of life. You are more than just a body or a human being living in a human world. YYou are a spiritual being with a physical vessel that has a social experience to assist you in expressing more of who you're. So whatever your empathic abilities are, embrace them from the perspective of the truth about who you're - whatever that means for you.

That's why earlier in this book I said my conviction is that all human beings have the capacity for empathy and depending on where they sit on that spectrum, we get to experience a little or a lot of their empathic abilities. Having determined that you sit high on that positive side of the spectrum, your special skills come into your human experience naturally, and it's your job to be grounded and intelligent enough to use them effectively.

Psychics, clairvoyants, and others with similar abilities aren't different from you, they've just fine-tuned their receptors in a specific way to access and interpret information that perhaps you haven't unlocked yet.

And you should never feel obliged to unlock anything your not comfortable with by the way, because being an empath doesn't automatically mean you need to be clairvoyant or psychic.

To some extent, your sensitivities and ability to connect with all the energies around you already makes you a natural psychic or clairvoyant. That's why you'll often receive a flashing thought, image or feeling of an old friend or family member that you haven't heard from in a while and all of a sudden they will call or communicate in some way. Whether you want to develop these into an actual skill that can be accurately used in the "psychic realm" is entirely up to you.

What is a psychic person?

This is a person who can supposedly receive information and communicate with spirits manifested as regular humans as well as spirits within the spirit realm. There is another psychic commonly referred to as a "psychic medium" who can supposedly communicate with discarnate spirits. In essence, such a person uses himself or herself as a means of communication (kind of like a telephone) to pass on messages from one spirit being to another.

What is a clairvoyant person?

This is a person who can see clearly with the mind's eye. Originally French, the term 'Clair' means 'clear,' and 'voyance' means 'vision' and it enables the individual in question to see events, people, scenarios and even places within their mind's eye.

Usually, the argument made is that psychics deal with thought energies while empaths deal with emotional energies but again, I want to get back to my earlier point.

The need to separate and dissect in this way only creates friction and confusion. After all, thought and emotions have an unbroken bond, why then attempt to pick a side? Rather than debate whether or not psychics, clairvoyants, and empaths are playing on the same team, focus on understanding more of your empathic abilities. Refrain from too much labeling, and I would recommend you refrain judgment around the debate of whether being an empath is linked to spirituality.

Understanding your intuition, healing powers and grounding yourself:

I think it's safe to say any empath with a strong, highly developed intuition and healing powers has already ventured into spirituality and higher consciousness. For we know, science can't be able to back up with concrete proof of how one can heal or soothe an animal in pain with just the touch of a hand. And I'm guessing they would've a hard time explaining how you're able to receive such strong intuitive messages that are almost always right on the money.

My friends and family have developed the habit of always having a conversation with me whenever they are faced with a major decision because my intuition has never failed to respond positively when summoned. If something feels off for me, I've learned to trust that information. Have you?

If yes, then you're currently experiencing the benefits of spiritually activating your empathic abilities. The good news is your intuitive abilities, natural healing potential, and a strong sense of groundedness will skyrocket once you open your mind and consciously connect to something higher than your current level of awareness.

The fact that you can sense the energy all around you means you can extend your awareness and sense the strength of our solar system, our galaxy, our universe. And as you connect to the power generating all these macrocosms, does it not make sense to seek the intelligence, wisdom, energy, and guidance that produces it all? That is where true spiritual awakening begins. And if that's something that resonates with you, I hope that you'll get curious enough to pull on the thread of spirituality and higher consciousness. See where that leads and how that empowers your life.

Before we conclude our journey together, I want to share practical tips that'll catapult you into that path of prosperity and personal fulfillment regardless of the work, relationships, and goals you set for yourself.

CHAPTER 10: QUICK PRACTICAL TIPS TO START THRIVING IN LIFE AS AN EMPATH

"The really important thing isn't to live, but to live well...and to live well means the same thing as to live honorably or rightly."

-Socrates

Inhale... Exhale. You've made it this far. Bask in the joyful feeling of accomplishment having journeyed with me to this last chapter. We are here to equip you with life tools that you can pick and choose as you see fit to help you navigate the path of creating a thriving lifestyle.

Tip One: Start putting yourself first

As an empath, this is counterintuitive, and yet I

promise you, learning to put yourself first will benefit everyone in your world. It sounds selfish and makes you question whether you're a terrible person. Yes, I know those tiny voices in our heads, but as I mentioned earlier, this will be part of the paradigm shifting and shedding of false belief systems. You aren't evil or selfish person when you make sure your needs are being met first before catering to the needs of others.

Do you know why in the plane the flight attendants always tell you to pull your oxygen mask first before assisting anyone else including your baby? Good. The same rule applies here. Your empathic abilities and heightened sensitivities only work when you're energized not when you're depleted.

There's an ancient proverb that says, " One can't pour from an empty cup." How true! That's what the flight attendants mean, and that's also what I mean. You need to be filled and energized at all times. Otherwise, you run the risk of being "filled" with whatever junk people are dealing with.

Some of the ways I recommend you start practicing this by:

Taking up yoga classes.

Learning to meditate daily or other mindfulness practices.

Take up daily devotionals or prayer time if that's your thing.

Create your own special rituals that help you practice self-love and self-care.

Give yourself special treats often. For example, I buy myself flowers, cupcakes, chocolate, or perfume often just because I know these gifts make me feel loved.

Can you think of one or two things you could do this week to make yourself feel loved?

Tip Two: Prioritize your emotions

As a highly sensitive person, you can process a lot of emotions in an instant. You deeply "feel" everything. Your emotions, thoughts, and sensations are pretty loud in your mind and heart. But it's not just your emotions; it's also everyone around you. That's where it can get tough because you might get so caught up helping others process their emotions that you end up numbing out yours.

Get into the habit of regularly doing a self-check. Check in with your emotional status at regular intervals to make sure they are working in service of your dreams and goals.

I also want you to work on developing filters so that you can stop automatically absorbing whatever comes into your world. Be more aware of how much information you consume and raise your radar so you can quickly pick up when someone's trying to use you as a sounding board for their dysfunctional lifestyle. I'm not saying to shut people out who need your advice. What I'm encouraging though, is that you set a time limit so that you don't get too immersed into their world to the point of drowning.

As an empath, you tend to get caught up in other people's energies and stories. As you absorb this, it becomes entangled with your own emotions, energies, and story than before you know it; your body, mind, and affairs start projecting lies that weren't even yours, to begin with. The universal language is emotions. The most dominant emotional state you hold is the communication the universe receives, and it'll reflect back to your conditions and circumstances that match your broadcast. Therefore, learn to master and better process your emotions.

This can be done informally or formally, but the most important thing is to remember that you'ren't meant to be an island. You can find ways that resonate with your personality and process your emotions in healthy habits.

If you're spiritually inclined, consider arranging talks with a spiritual leader.

Do you enjoy journaling? Then buy a special book for recording your emotions and have transferred all that inner dialogue onto paper every night before sleeping.

If you like being part of a group or community, then join a group counseling session near you.

You could also find a trained therapist or a life coach and do monthly sessions.

If you have a partner or friend, you can trust, then organize weekly coffee dates to speak about your emotions and what you're currently feeling.

These are just a few of endless options to test out. Which option will you choose to help you build your emotional support structure?

Tip Three: Practice gratitude religiously

Although many people talk about the high sensitivity and feeling nature of the empaths, it's usually in reference to pain and sadness. But you and I both know we feel joy and pleasure just as profoundly and it's these joyful experiences that we need to capitalize on more.

In the same way all wellbeing experts advice us to create mindfulness rituals to help take care of the mind, body, and soul, we also need to develop routines that help us anchor in the deep feeling of gratitude, appreciation, and celebration.

There is so much power in the practice of gratitude. It has been taught for centuries across various religions and philosophies, and modern science has proven the biological benefits of praise and appreciation. I know some people struggle with creating a daily practice out of this, so try a few things and stick to the one that feels most enriching to you. Remember it's about cultivating that feeling and creating that deep connection.

Buy a beautiful journal and name it " my gratitude journal" where you document 3-5 things daily you feel good about.

Download a gratitude app and use that instead just before you start the day.

Take yourself out on a particular date to celebrate being you.

Send a thank you note of thoughtful gift each week to at least one person in your life that you appreciate.

Tip Four: Get enough sleep and downtime

Arianna Huffington founder of Thrive Global is an ambassador for sleep. She believes that everything you do, you'll do better with a good night's sleep. In her book titled The sleep Revolution, Arianna says, "By assisting us in maintaining the world in perspective, sleep provides us with an opportunity to refocus on who we are. And in that link destination, dropping away is simpler for the world's fears and worries."

We live in a sleep-deprived community where little to no sleep proves that one is more hardworking and active in the community. Well, thanks to advocates like Arianna, the world is starting to realize the harmful effects of inadequate sleep. For empaths, this is doubly important because we absorb and process so much. Comprising the quality and quantity of sleep that our bodies need to operate at optimum levels is part of the reason we try so much to cope with a demanding world. I don't know about you, but without my 8 hours of restful sleep, my mind feels so scattered, noisy, and overwhelmed. My ability to calmly direct my energy is significantly reduced. So I've learned the hard way to stop messing with my sleep, and I encourage you to do the same.

Alongside getting adequate restful sleep, give yourself time to relax and unwind after a busy day. When you attend public events, meetings, or travel, make sure you set aside time to relax in quietness so you can lower your stimulation levels and restore your sanity.

How much sleep do you usually get? Is it high-quality, restful sleep? What are a few changes you can make to ensure you get optimum rest each night?

Tip Five: Find your purpose and vision and follow it

Find something that excites and invigorates you and pursue it with all your might. Don't wait for something to fall on your lap one day. Each moment of your life is a moment you'll never get back. You get to decide whether your life is going to be created by design or by default.

In essence, as long as you're breathing, you'll be creating. And the sooner you start being the grand architect of your life and make up a vision that makes you happy, the sooner you can start moving in the direction where you'll feel fulfilled and satisfied.

Ever heard the old saying "without a vision, the people perish"?

That's what happens to your powers, your sense of aliveness, and your dreams. They perish without a clear vision from you. If you genuinely want to be an empowered empath who thrives in this modern world, you must create a vision and figure out what makes you feel good. Even if you don't yet know what your purpose is or how to use your gifts, things will fall into place as you follow the path of your pure bliss.

It takes boldness and determination, but I know you can do it. Here's your first baby step. Answer this question honestly, with great feeling and without reservation.

What would I love to be, do, and have in this life?

Tip six: Develop a gentle way of dealing with both internal and external conflict

Our experience of conflict, especially with a loved one is unbearable. We can't stand that horrid feeling and inner battle that arises whenever a disagreement occurs, which is probably why most empaths keep everything in. Having to deal with anger is also not easy for us, plus we hate the thought of hurting someone else because we know how awful that feels.

Here's the thing though. You've done it all your life. You are going along with something just for the sake of it even if it hurts you - avoiding conflict and confrontation at all cost. Has this choice made you a happier person?

I'm not suggesting you become a drama queen or king. Tantrums never resolve anything. But I do want to encourage you to find healthy ways of dealing with disagreement and conflict without absorbing the negative energy and letting it slowly consume you. Running away isn't the best solution because there's also the inner conflict that often invades to which you have no escape. So my suggestion is simple.

Find exercises, techniques, and practices that help you courageously face and resolve conflicts in healthy ways.

Techniques like the verbal Aikido I shared earlier or the STOP method that world-renowned personal transformation leader Dr. Deepak Chopra teaches. S.T.O.P is an acronym for:

1. Stop what you're doing.
2. Take three deep breaths and smile with your whole body.
3. Observe what's happening and what you're feeling in your mind and body.
4. Proceed with loving kindness and compassion.

In any given situation, you have the power to practice STOP. Instead of running away from an uncomfortable situation or a brewing inner or outer conflict, test this technique and notice what begins to happen to your sense of empowerment.

Stepping into your power as an empath when amid a crisis, conflict or chaos is perhaps the best gift you could ever give the world and yourself. It will take practice and self-discipline, but if you're ready to be a powerful force for good in the world, you'll master and overcome all obstacles that stand in the way of you growing your empathic powers including conflict and chaos.

What are some things you could start training yourself to do whenever a conflict arises?

Tip seven: Take up Yoga or Pilates

Both are forms of exercise that go beyond physical exercising. They are especially useful because they combine breathing, centering, and grounding all the while strengthening your body. It's an amazing way to feel wonderful and raise your vibrational state even if you do fifteen minutes in the comfort of your home.

Tip Eight: Set aside time daily for self-awareness

What is self-awareness? This is your ability to go within and become consciously aware of your thoughts, feelings, physical sensations, and behaviors.

This is usually tough for empaths because we tend to be layered up by other people's needs, thought patterns, and energies, which is why you need to do this as a daily ritual. Set a specific time where it's not for physical exercise or meditation but merely a time to be with yourself, listening to yourself, observing that which is presently taking place deep within until you become more familiar with your true voice and feelings.

For example, when I shared the story of how I was smitten by this guy yet at the end of spending a weekend together I would curl up in bed completely drained and almost feeling sickly, that particular Sunday when I "caught myself" curled up in the same position experiencing the same sensations six Sundays in a row was my moment of self-awareness. I became aware of my forming habit and realized something was off. If you make this self-awareness time a regular or daily practice, it won't take you six weeks to realize you're going down the wrong rabbit hole! Now I know better, and my life has changed thanks to self-awareness.

A simple way to start is by doing some mirror work, as this will give you direct insight into how you perceive yourself, thereby increasing self-awareness.

Tip Nine: Fortify your intuitive guidance system.

Work on fortifying your intuitive abilities. The more your nurture and learn to trust it, the clearer the information becomes. There is no better direction on your path to help you sense when you're going down a dark rabbit hole than your intuition. It will save you time, heartache, and even protect you from energy vampires and narcissist.

Your intuition will also amplify your healing powers and enable you to sense when someone you care about needs help even before they say it. It will always be the more calm, quiet voice, pay attention to it, and don't allow pride or the ego distract you from receiving and taking action on the guidance given.

Daily mindfulness practices such as heart meditation, transcendental meditation, and mindful breathing will strengthen you and offer exceptional clarity. Taking even three minutes out of your day to practice deep breathing techniques isn't only good for your body, but it also keeps anxiety and stress at bay. Being mindful is one of the greatest gifts you can give yourself; use it to your advantage.

Tip Eleven: Soothe yourself using positive self-talk and conscious breath work

This is especially useful if you realize some unhealthy behaviors impulsively take over whenever a stress trigger occurs. In such cases, take a few deep and prolonged breaths doing your best to center yourself in your body. Allow yourself to feel your body and all the sensations even if they are unwanted. Using positive self-talk, speak words either aloud or mentally that offer you a sense of relief at that moment. Do not try to reach for words that are too far-fetched or that sound "made up." Stick to whatever resonates with you at that moment and makes you feel better.

For one person, a little motivational pep talk might be the right answer, and for another, it could be a more holy statement like "This too shall pass. Peace is still." I don't know what it'll be for you but get into the habit of being your best cheerleader, and this practice will become highly effective when stress hits.

Tip Twelve: Try Aromatherapy and essential oils

Our ability to process and connect with energies, smells, and other stimuli can be overwhelming, but we can also use it to our edge. If you enjoy essential oils, test out aromatherapy as an alternative to helping you de-stress and calm your nerves.

When we inhale the aroma of oils that resonate with us, it can immediately kick our body into action, causing the production of hormones like serotonin and dopamine. Just make sure you pick and choose the oils that ignite and de-stress you.

YOUR NEXT BEST STEP:

It's time to plan out the new story of your life. What kind of a lifestyle would you love to own 12 months from now?

Regardless of what people say around you, the world has always been a mix of good and bad. Duality is what makes human living enjoyable. Darkness and light must co-exist for us to become conscious of what light is.

Therefore you'll continue to hear mixed reviews and debates around whether what you possess is a gift or a curse and to be fair, you could spend the rest of your life a happy empath, or a miserable burdened coping empath, barely surviving, and the universe couldn't care less. So this is a matter of perspective and mindset.

You will have to choose how to show up in the world and the image you want to live up to. The secret to living a life that's fulfilling, meaningful, and joyful as an empath is simple: Personal evolution is what you need.

Develop a new lifestyle plan that's grounded and customized for your evolution:

For you to successfully create a blueprint for a life you love living; you'll need to engage...

- Your Imagination
- Your Attention
- Your Intention

Without these three things, no amount of planning strategizing or designing will amount to tangible results. Let's see how they will impact your blueprint.

Imagination - The best use of your imagination is to start designing the kind of future you would love to experience. What would you like to experience?

Who would you love to be? Can you vividly see this new you?

Do your best to connect emotionally and visually with this new self that's longing to be made real. The more you can connect with that new you, the easier it'll be to ascertain the details necessary to make your lifestyle blueprint work.

Attention - Where attention goes, energy flows. It's that simple. If your focus is on growth, more considerable expansion, and personal evolution, your energy will become more concentrated along those lines, and your life will continue to expand in that direction.

Intention - Be more intentional with your desire to grow and evolve. As Napoleon Hill said, the reference point of all great feat is a burning desire. For you to have a thriving lifestyle, increase your success, health, wealth, and love in your life, you must desire to be something other than what you currently are. Making the intention that you desire to bring forth a new version of yourself and stepping into every situation each day with that intention will start to propel your life in a different direction because again, the universe is always listening and responding to the energy you broadcast.

What you need is more orderliness brought back into your daily life. You need more clarity, and you need to permit yourself to become the architect of your life and energy.

If you're not into goal setting, that's okay. I'm not asking you to set goals here; I'm asking you to become the author of your book of life. It's time to start a new chapter filled with magical meaningful moments, adventure, maybe even romance and a lot of difference-making in the world.

The only one who can author this book is you.

With a long list of practical tools for life, tips on how to soothe yourself and handle nasty situations, you have everything you need to begin a new chapter of your life. Only the stories you tell yourself can hold you back. And the best way to prevent an old tale from blocking you is to write up a new story. Focus on the journey itself, the meaningful experiences that you wish to encounter, and the process, not the goals.

A simple exercise that usually helps kick things off when designing a lifestyle blueprint is a process called clarity through contrast. Grab an A4 paper and create two columns. On the left, label that side things that cause me to contract and self-sabotage. On the right, label it things I'll focus on for greater expansion.

An example would be jotting down on the left "lack of sleep" if you know that's one of the'ssues you want to improve in this new chapter and then, of course, the new story would be "restful and adequate sleeping routine."

At the end of this exercise, you'll have all the old things that have kept you stuck and living a mediocre life on the left, and you'll have to the right all the wonderful new experiences that await you as you step into this new chapter of your life.

A few helpful things to help you craft your lifestyle in case you're feeling a bit lost on what kinds of experiences would constitute an expanding, empowered life as an empath include:

- Receiving more love.
- Giving more love, compassion, goodwill, etc.
- Being of service.
- Meditating daily.
- Finding creative channels.
- Interacting more with nature.
- Using your gifts at work.

- Doing more things that bring you joy and the feeling of fun.

This list is endless, but I hope you're getting the picture. By the time you're done putting a vivid, descriptive lifestyle plan of how your life will feel like and be in the next 12 months, some or all of these things on the list as well as others I'ven't mentioned will all be included in that blueprint. And that'll become the preview of what you can expect moving forward.

Be comfortable when things get uncomfortable.

I don't want to leave you with the impression that the journey to this new lifestyle will be all unicorns and rainbows. It's bound to get uncomfortable, and that's when you'll have to step things up. Part of having this documented blueprint is to have a guiding reminder and reference point to use whenever things get crappy, and you wonder why you're even making all these changes.

You've got to learn to be comfortable with the uncomfortable, and you've got to find ways to keep yourself accountable so that you don't fall back into the old story. That's where things like community, coaching, and mentorship come into play. Different options work best for different people. There is no one size fits all. Any of them could work for you as long as you figure out which one best meets your needs and you take action on that decision. The only way to being an empowered empath is getting on that path yourself, and it does begin with that inner work that you commit to doing. Permit yourself to create a new story and a new life that'll benefit you and all of humanity!

www.ingramcontent.com/pod-product-compliance
Lightning Source LLC
Chambersburg PA
CBHW060400080526
44583CB00012B/408